Buckle Down™

Pennsylvania
Mathematics

Level 4

2nd Edition

This book belongs to: _____

Buckle Down
Publishing

Helping your schoolhouse meet the standards of the statehouse™

ISBN 0-7836-5491-X

2BDPA04MM01   4 5 6 7 8 9 10

Senior Editor: Todd Hamer; Project Editor: Rob Hill; Production Editor: Jennifer Rapp; Cover Design: Christina Nantz; Cover Graphic Designer: Christina Kroemer; Production Director: Jennifer Booth; Art Director: Chris Wolf; Graphic Designer: Spike Schabacker; Composition: Wyndham Books.

Cover image: © Steve Allen/Brand X Pictures/Jupiterimages

TABLE OF CONTENTS

To the Teacher:

"Eligible Content" codes are listed for each lesson in the table of contents and for each page in the shaded gray bar that runs across the tops of the pages in the workbook (see example to the right). These codes indicate which Eligible Content are covered in a given lesson or on a given page.

Introduction

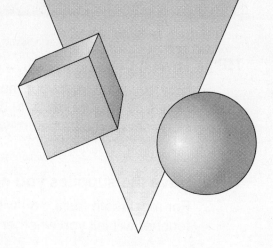

When you start thinking about all of the times and places you use your math skills, you might be surprised. How many minutes are left until school is over for the day? How much taller are you now than you were a year ago? How many points per game is the leading scorer for the Philadelphia 76ers averaging? These are examples of how people use math every day.

This book will help you practice your everyday math skills. It will also help you with math that is more uncommon, like the kinds you might only see in math class and on math tests. If you practice all the math skills in this book, you will be ready to do your best on almost any math test.

Test-Taking Tips

Here are a few tips that will help you on test day.

TIP 1: Take it easy.

Stay calm and trust your math skills. You've practiced the problems in *Buckle Down*, so you are ready to do your best on almost any math test. Take a few slow, deep breaths before you begin the test.

TIP 2: Have the supplies you need.

For most math tests, you will need two sharp pencils and an eraser. Your teacher will tell you whether you need anything else.

TIP 3: Read the questions more than once.

Every question is different. Some questions are more difficult than others. If you need to, read a question more than once. This will help you make a plan for solving the problem.

TIP 4: Learn to "plug in" answers to multiple-choice items.

When do you "plug in"? You should "plug in" whenever your answer is different from all of the answer choices or you can't come up with an answer. Plug each answer choice into the problem and find the one that makes sense. (You can also think of this as "working backwards.")

TIP 5: Check your work.

Take the time to check your work on every problem. By checking your work, you can find and fix careless mistakes.

TIP 6: Use all the test time.

Work on the test until you are told to stop. If you finish early, go back through the test and double-check your answers. You just might improve your score on the test by finding and fixing any errors you might have made.

TIP 7: Answer open-ended items completely.

When answering open-ended items, show all your work to receive as many points as possible. Write neatly enough so that your work will be easy to follow. Make sure your answer is clearly marked.

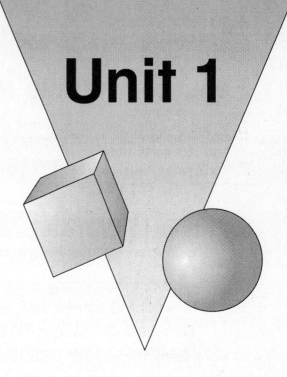

Unit 1

Numbers and Operations

You may not realize it, but you use your number sense many times a day. You solve problems using numbers when you figure out how much time you have to get ready for school, about how much money you will need for a Philadelphia Eagles ticket, or if it will be warm enough to go swimming. Having number sense helps you to understand things such as time, money, and temperature. Numbers are important in every part of your life.

In this unit, you will solve problems involving addition, subtraction, multiplication, and division. You will learn about whole numbers, decimals, and fractions. You will also learn strategies for problem solving.

In This Unit

Whole Numbers

Decimals

Fractions and Mixed
   Numbers

Estimation and Problem
   Solving

Lesson 1: Whole Numbers

A **whole number** is a number that shows ones, tens, hundreds, and so on. You can write a whole number using digits, words, or drawings. In this lesson, you will write numbers in different forms. You will also compute with whole numbers.

Digits and Words

0, 1, 2, 3, 4, 5, 6, 7, 8, and 9 are the **digits** used to write whole numbers.

The number 1,247 has four digits: 1   2   4   7

The number 1,247 is written in **standard form**.

In **word form**, the number 1,247 is written: **one thousand, two hundred forty-seven**.

Using Commas

Commas separate groups of digits so that you can easily read large numbers. You can't put commas just anywhere in a large number, however.

Example

Put a comma in the correct place in the number 923184.

Start at the far right of the number. Work your way left. Place a comma to the left of every 3rd digit.

$$9 \; 2 \; 3 , 1 \; 8 \; 4 \; \leftarrow \text{start}$$
$$ \; 2 \quad 1 \quad 3 \quad 2 \quad 1$$

Written with a comma, the number 923184 is 923,184.

Eligible Content: M4.A.1.1.4

Place Value

Place-value tables show the values of the digits in a number.

 Example

This place-value table shows the values of the digits of 891,247.

Hundred Thousands	Ten Thousands	Thousands	Hundreds	Tens	Ones
8	9	1	2	4	7

Numbers written in **expanded form** show the values of the digits.

891,247 = 800,000 + 90,000 + 1,000 + 200 + 40 + 7

 Example

This place-value table shows the values of the digits of 308,041.

Hundred Thousands	Ten Thousands	Thousands	Hundreds	Tens	Ones
3	0	8	0	4	1

Notice that there are no ten thousands or hundreds in 308,041. This is why a **0 (zero)** is written in each of those places. Zeros are not shown in expanded form or written in word form.

308,041 = 300,000 + 8,000 + 40 + 1

308,041 = three hundred eight thousand, forty-one

   ↑   ↑—**hundreds**

ten thousands

Practice

1. Write the digits of the following numbers in the correct places in the table.

54,736   498,039   5,973

Hundred Thousands	Ten Thousands	Thousands	Hundreds	Tens	Ones

Directions: For Numbers 2 through 4, write the numbers in expanded form and word form.

2. 54,736

   expanded form _____

   word form _____

3. 498,039

   expanded form _____

   word form _____

4. 5,973

   expanded form _____

   word form _____

5. What is the standard form of seven hundred thirty thousand, four hundred eighty-two?

   A. 73,482

   B. 700,482

   C. 703,482

   D. 730,482

6. What is the standard form of one hundred eight thousand, four hundred?

   A. 18,400

   B. 81,400

   C. 108,400

   D. 801,400

Eligible Content: M4.A.1.2.2

Comparing and Ordering Whole Numbers

When you compare two numbers, you decide which number is **greater than** the other or which number is **less than** the other. Sometimes when you compare two numbers, you find that the numbers are **equal**.

Signs for Comparison

The signs that are used to compare numbers are >, <, and =.

> means **is greater than**

< means **is less than**

= means **is equal to**

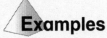 **Examples**

47 is greater than 46, so 47 > 46.

15 is less than 28, so 15 < 28.

34 is equal to 34, so 34 = 34.

 Practice

Directions: For Numbers 1 through 12, use >, <, or = to compare the whole numbers.

1. 32 _____ 5

2. 48 _____ 39

3. 56 _____ 48

4. 732 _____ 793

5. 938 _____ 928

6. 451,072 _____ 451,072

7. 26 _____ 31

8. 25,617 _____ 25,671

9. 9,278 _____ 8,928

10. 5,782 _____ 5,872

11. 820,950 _____ 802,905

12. 469 _____ 496

Place-value Tables

You can use place-value tables to compare and order whole numbers. Compare the digits in each place-value position from left to right, and look for the first place-value position where the digits are different.

Example

In the following table, the numbers have the same digits in the hundred-thousands and ten-thousands places. The digits are different in the thousands place.

Hundred Thousands	Ten Thousands	Thousands	Hundreds	Tens	Ones
3	4	**4**	3	2	7
3	4	**2**	4	7	1
3	4	**7**	1	5	2

The digit 4 is greater than the digit 2, so **344,327 > 342,471**.

The digit 2 is less than the digit 7, so **342,471 < 347,152**.

The digit 4 is less than the digit 7, so **344,327 < 347,152**.

Example

Write the numbers from the table above in order from **greatest** to **least**.

Because 347,152 is greater than each of the other two numbers, it is the greatest number.

Because 342,471 is less than each of the other two numbers, it is the least number.

The numbers written in order from **greatest** to **least** are 347,152; 344,327; 342,471.

Eligible Content: M4.A.1.2.2

 **Practice**

Directions: Use the following table to answer Numbers 1 through 4.

Hundred Thousands	Ten Thousands	Thousands	Hundreds	Tens	Ones
9	4	2	8	6	1
9	4	4	4	6	3
9	4	3	9	2	7

1. What is the first place-value position in which the digits are different?

   _____

2. Which number from the table is the **greatest**? _____

3. Which number from the table is the **least**? _____

4. Write the numbers from the table in order from **least** to **greatest**.

   _____

Directions: For Numbers 5 and 6, write the whole numbers in order from **least** to **greatest**.

5. 3,648   4,958   3,701   3,835 _____

6. 54,258   52,825   52,582   53,867 _____

Directions: For Numbers 7 and 8, write the whole numbers in order from **greatest** to **least**.

7. 482,429   484,325   483,802 _____

8. 852,619   873,481   862,983 _____

Addition

The answer to an addition problem is the **sum**. The numbers that are added are **addends**. To find the sum, line up the digits with the same place values. Remember to "regroup" when necessary.

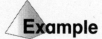 **Example**

Add: 158,252 + 362,495

Line up the place values.

```
  158,252
+ 362,495
```

Add the ones.

```
  158,252
+ 362,495
        7
```

Add the tens. Regroup the hundreds.

```
     1
  158,252
+ 362,495
       47
```

Add the hundreds.

```
     1
  158,252
+ 362,495
      747
```

Add the thousands. Regroup the ten thousands.

```
    1 1
  158,252
+ 362,495
    0,747
```

Eligible Content: M4.A.2.1.1

Add the ten thousands. Regroup the hundred thousands.

```
  11  1
  158,252
+ 362,495
───────────
   20,747
```

Add the hundred thousands.

```
  11  1
  158,252
+ 362,495
───────────
  520,747
```

$$158,252 + 362,495 = 520,747$$

Because addition and subtraction are **inverse** (opposite) **operations**, you can use subtraction to check your answer.

When you subtract one of the addends from the sum, you should get the other addend.

```
4 1110 6 14              4 1110 6 14
  520,747                  520,747
− 362,495                − 158,252
───────────              ───────────
  158,252                  362,495
```

Your answer is correct.

Example

Pennsylvania has 44,820 square miles of land and 1,239 square miles of water. What is the total area of the land and water combined?

```
regroup the thousands digit →   1
                              44,820
                            +  1,239
                            ───────────
                              46,059
```

The total area of Pennsylvania is 46,059 square miles.

Practice

Directions: For Numbers 1 through 10, line up the digits with the same place values, and then add.

1. 95 + 33 = _____

2. 467 + 1,286 = _____

3. 5,297 + 2,031 = _____

4. 406,975 + 100,213 = _____

5. 791 + 916 = _____

6. 21,023 + 17,008 = _____

7. 1,554 + 848 = _____

8. 27 + 1,974 = _____

9. 624 + 1,208 = _____

10. 463 + 20,807 = _____

Eligible Content: M4.A.2.1.1

Directions: For Numbers 11 through 15, use addition to find the answer.

11. Drew drove 134 miles from Allentown to Williamsport. Then he drove 261 miles from Williamsport to Erie. How far did Drew drive in all?

    _____

12. According to the 2000 census, Altoona, Pennsylvania, had a population of 49,523. Wilkes-Barre, Pennsylvania, had a population of 43,123. What is the population of the two cities combined?

    _____

13. Hannah and Emma are both selling cookies. Hannah has sold 105 cookies, and Emma has sold 79 cookies. How many cookies have they sold in all?

    _____

14. Penn Elementary has 736 students. Franklin Elementary has 591 students. How many students are at the two schools altogether?

    _____

15. Two fourth-grade classes at Liberty Elementary collected cans to recycle. One class collected 1,045 cans, and the other class collected 1,309 cans. How many cans did the two classes collect altogether?

    _____

Eligible Content: M4.A.2.1.1

Subtraction

The answer to a subtraction problem is called the **difference**. When finding the difference, remember to borrow and regroup when needed.

 Example

Subtract: 625,189 − 353,242

Line up the place values.

$$
\begin{array}{r}
625{,}189 \\
-\ 353{,}242 \\
\hline
\end{array}
$$

Subtract the ones.

$$
\begin{array}{r}
625{,}189 \\
-\ 353{,}242 \\
\hline
7
\end{array}
$$

Subtract the tens.

$$
\begin{array}{r}
625{,}189 \\
-\ 353{,}242 \\
\hline
47
\end{array}
$$

Borrow 1 thousand. Then subtract the hundreds.

$$
\begin{array}{r}
{}^{4\ 11} \\
62\cancel{5}{,}\cancel{1}89 \\
-\ 353{,}242 \\
\hline
947
\end{array}
$$

Subtract the thousands.

$$
\begin{array}{r}
{}^{4\ 11} \\
62\cancel{5}{,}\cancel{1}89 \\
-\ 353{,}242 \\
\hline
1{,}947
\end{array}
$$

Eligible Content: M4.A.2.1.1

Borrow 1 hundred thousand. Then subtract the ten thousands.

```
    5 12 4 11
    6̷2̷5̷,1̷89
  −  353,242
     7 1,947
```

Subtract the hundred thousands.

```
    5 12 4 11
    6̷2̷5̷,1̷89
  −  353,242
    271,947
```

$$625,189 - 353,242 = 271,947$$

Because subtraction and addition are inverse operations, you can use addition to check your answer.

When you add the difference and the number you subtracted, you should get the number you subtracted from.

```
     1  1
    271,947
  +  353,242
    625,189
```

Your answer is correct.

Example

There were 35,634 fans at the beginning of a Pitt Panthers football game. By the end of the game there were 17,022 fans. How many fans left the game before it was over?

```
                        2 15
borrow and regroup  →  3̷5̷,634
                     −  17,022
                        18,612
```

There were 18,612 fans that left the game.

Eligible Content: M4.A.2.1.1

Practice

Directions: For Numbers 1 through 10, line up the digits with the same place values, and then subtract.

1. 4,793 – 1,475 = _____

2. 25,080 – 20,457 = _____

3. 95 – 13 = _____

4. 702,986 – 48,408 = _____

5. 407 – 192 = _____

6. 1,825 – 872 = _____

7. 74,120 – 59,564 = _____

8. 4,420 – 2,183 = _____

9. 92,553 – 7,804 = _____

10. 8,271 – 368 = _____

Directions: For Numbers 11 through 15, use subtraction to find the answer.

11. According to the 2000 census, Reading, Pennsylvania, had a population of 81,207. Bethlehem, Pennsylvania, had a population of 71,329. How many more people lived in Reading than in Bethlehem?

   _____

12. It is 761 miles from Philadelphia, Pennsylvania, to Chicago, Illinois. It is 2,393 miles from Philadelphia to Phoenix, Arizona. From Philadelphia, how many more miles is it to Phoenix than to Chicago?

   _____

13. Elijah is 3,390 days old. His brother Ehud is 4,770 days old. How many days older than Elijah is Ehud?

   _____

14. In the 2007 regular season, Ben Roethlisberger had 3,154 passing yards for the Pittsburgh Steelers. In 2006, he had 3,513 passing yards. How many more passing yards did Ben Roethlisberger have in 2006 than in 2007?

   _____

15. Ellen's school district has 52,816 students and 4,034 teachers. How many more students are there than teachers?

   _____

Eligible Content: M4.A.2.1.1

Multiplication

Multiplication is a shortcut for repeated addition. The answer to a multiplication problem is a **product**. The numbers you multiply are **factors**.

$$3 \times 4 = 12$$

factors   product

Example

One level of a parking garage can hold 275 cars. There are 8 levels in the parking garage. How many cars can the parking garage hold?

Line up the digits with the same place values. Remember, multiplying 275 × 8 is like adding 275 groups of 8.

```
    275
  ×   8
```

Multiply the ones by 8: 5 × 8 = 40. Write a 0 and carry the 4 extra tens.

```
    4
    275
  ×   8
    0
```

Multiply the tens by 8: 7 tens × 8 = 56 tens. Then add the 4 tens to the 56 tens: 4 + 56 = 60. Write a 0 and carry the 6 extra hundreds.

```
  6 4
    275
  ×   8
    00
```

Multiply the hundreds by 8: 2 hundreds × 8 = 16 hundreds. Then add the 6 hundreds to the 16 hundreds: 6 + 16 = 22. Write a 2 and carry the 2 extra thousands. Write a 2 in the thousands place.

```
  6 4
    275
  ×   8
  2,200
```

The parking garage can hold 2,200 cars.

 TIP: You can use division to check the answer to a multiplication problem.

Practice

Directions: For Numbers 1 through 10, line up the factors, then find the product.

1. $197 \times 4 = $ _____

6. $99 \times 9 = $ _____

2. $579 \times 6 = $ _____

7. $353 \times 2 = $ _____

3. $38 \times 8 = $ _____

8. $855 \times 3 = $ _____

4. $483 \times 5 = $ _____

9. $46 \times 7 = $ _____

5. $212 \times 5 = $ _____

10. $92 \times 5 = $ _____

Directions: For Numbers 11 through 15, use multiplication to find the answer.

11. Damon can drive 23 miles on 1 gallon of gas. How many miles can Damon drive on 7 gallons of gas?

    _____

12. The dinosaur triceratops had 3 horns. How many horns could you find in a herd of 85 triceratops?

    _____

13. Alcott Elementary School has 3 fourth-grade classes. If each class has 24 students, how many fourth graders are there at Alcott Elementary?

    _____

14. A wagon holds 103 bales of hay. There are 9 wagons. How many bales of hay are there?

    _____

15. Aidan's mom keeps a photo album of their family pictures. The album has 70 pages and each page has 4 photos. How many photos are in the album?

    _____

Eligible Content: M4.A.1.3.2

Multiples

When you multiply two whole numbers, the product is a **multiple** of both numbers.

 Example

What are the multiples of 4?

You need to find the product of 4 and each of the whole numbers.

$4 \times 0 = 0$ $4 \times 3 = 12$

$4 \times 1 = 4$ $4 \times 4 = 16$

$4 \times 2 = 8$ $4 \times 5 = 20$ and so on . . .

The multiples of 4 are 0, 4, 8, 12, 16, 20, and so on.

Practice

Directions: For Numbers 1 through 3, fill in the missing multiples.

1. Multiples of **3**:   0, _____, 6, 9, 12, _____, 18, 21, 24, 27, _____, _____

2. Multiples of **5**:   0, 5, 10, _____, 20, 25, _____, 35, _____, _____, 50, 55

3. Multiples of **9**:   0, 9, 18, _____, 36, _____, 54, _____, _____, 81, _____, 99

4. What are the first ten multiples of 10?

_____

5. A postcard company makes postcards in packages of 8. Which number of postcards could Ken have bought?

   A. 22

   B. 56

   C. 90

   D. 98

6. An office supply store sells pencils in groups of 7. Which of these is **not** a number of pencils Katie could have bought?

   A. 56

   B. 78

   C. 84

   D. 98

Division

You can use division to split a set of objects into same-sized groups. You can also use division to find the number of objects in each same-sized group. The answer to a division problem is the **quotient**. The number you are dividing by is the **divisor**. The number you are dividing into is the **dividend**. The number that is left over, if there is one, is the **remainder**. Here are two ways to write division facts:

quotient → 4
divisor → 6)24
↑
dividend

24 ÷ 6 = 4 ← quotient
   ↑   ↑
dividend divisor

 **Example**

Mrs. Chu has 225 cookies to divide among 7 friends. How many cookies will each friend get? How many cookies will be left over?

Choose a way to write the problem.

7)225

Divide and multiply.

```
       3   ← How many 7's in 22?
   7)225
  −  21   ← Multiply: 7 × 3 = 21
```

Subtract and bring down the next number.

```
       3
   7)225
  −  21↓
      15
```

Divide, multiply, and subtract again.

```
      32   ← How many 7's in 15?
   7)225
  −  21↓
      15
  −   14  ← Multiply: 7 × 2 = 14
       1  ← The remainder (R) must be less than the divisor.
```

Each friend will get 32 cookies. There will be 1 cookie left over.

 TIP: You can use multiplication to check the answer to a division problem.

Eligible Content: M4.A.2.1.1

Practice

Directions: For Numbers 1 through 10, line up the divisor and the dividend, then find the quotient and the remainder, if there is one.

1. 270 ÷ 3 = _____

2. 235 ÷ 7 = _____

3. 505 ÷ 5 = _____

4. 487 ÷ 2 = _____

5. 448 ÷ 3 = _____

6. 2,142 ÷ 6 = _____

7. 853 ÷ 5 = _____

8. 816 ÷ 8 = _____

9. 6,372 ÷ 9 = _____

10. 5,690 ÷ 4 = _____

Directions: For Numbers 11 through 15, use division to find the answer.

11. There are 252 students at an elementary school near York, Pennsylvania. There are 9 classroom teachers. Each teacher has the same number of students in his or her class. How many students are in each class?

    _____

12. Bobby has 94 baseball cards. He wants to divide them into 5 equal stacks. How many stacks of baseball cards can Bobby make? How many baseball cards will be left over?

    _____

13. There are 14 students playing soccer at recess at Quaker Elementary. They are divided into 2 equal teams. How many students are on each team?

    _____

14. An area of land covers 152 acres. The land is divided into 4 farms. If all 4 farms are the same size, how many acres is each farm?

    _____

15. Mrs. Steele has 3 candy jars in her classroom. If she has 298 pieces of candy to split equally among the jars, how many pieces of candy will be in each jar? How many pieces of candy will be left over?

    _____

Eligible Content: M4.A.1.3.1

Factors

When you can divide a greater number by a lesser number evenly (with no remainder), the lesser number is a **factor** of the greater number.

Example

What are all the factors of 6?

You need to find all the numbers that divide 6 evenly.

$6 \div 1 = 6$	$6 \div 3 = 2$	$6 \div 5 = 1 \text{ R1}$
$6 \div 2 = 3$	$6 \div 4 = 1 \text{ R2}$	$6 \div 6 = 1$

The numbers 1, 2, 3, and 6 are the factors of 6.

Practice

Directions: For Numbers 1 through 4, list the factors of the given number.

1. 8 _____

2. 10 _____

3. 9 _____

4. 4 _____

5. Mario spent exactly $20 on video rentals. Which of these could **not** have been the price of each video?

   A. 10

   B. 6

   C. 4

   D. 2

6. Amanda divided 16 brownies evenly among her siblings. Which could be the number of brownies each sibling received?

   A. 9

   B. 6

   C. 4

   D. 3

MATHEMATICS

1. Which set of numbers is in order from **least** to **greatest**?

   A   39,312   39,132   39,231

   B   39,132   39,231   39,312

   C   39,231   39,312   39,132

   D   39,312   39,231   39,132

2. A movie theater sold 5,038 tickets in one week. What is the word form of 5,038?

   A   five hundred thirty-eight

   B   five thousand three hundred eight

   C   five thousand thirty-eight

   D   five thousand three hundred eighty

3. Add:

   $$387 + 265$$

   A   652

   B   642

   C   552

   D   542

4. Multiply:

   $$205 \times 9$$

   A   214

   B   1,145

   C   1,805

   D   1,845

5. What is thirty-four thousand, three hundred one in standard form?

   A   3,431

   B   34,031

   C   34,301

   D   304,301

6. Which list contains 3 multiples of 6?

   A   3, 6, 12

   B   6, 18, 30

   C   12, 24, 46

   D   16, 26, 36

7. What is 204,507 in expanded form?

   A   200,000 + 4,000 + 500 + 7

   B   2,000 + 400 + 500 + 7

   C   200,000 + 40,000 + 500 + 7

   D   20,000 + 4,000 + 500 + 7

MATHEMATICS

8. Which has the **greatest** value?

A 68,351

B 68,513

C 68,315

D 68,153

9. Subtract:

$$715,358 - 243,582$$

A 471,776

B 472,876

C 571,776

D 572,876

10. Which number is **less** than 534,825?

A 534,799

B 543,825

C 534,826

D 534,925

11. Which of the following is correct?

A $234 < 143$

B $2,451 > 2,514$

C $1,738 = 738$

D $897 < 978$

12. For a fund-raiser, Washington Elementary collected 19,383 box tops. Adams Elementary collected 45,093 box tops. How many box tops did the two schools collect together?

A 54,376

B 54,476

C 64,376

D 64,476

13. Mr. Roy is buying boxes of lightbulbs. Each box contains exactly 12 lightbulbs. Which could be the number of lightbulbs Mr. Roy is buying?

A 26

B 42

C 58

D 72

14. Jay planted 24 flowers in his flower garden. He planted them in rows. Each row has the same number of flowers. Which of these could be the number of flowers in each row?

A 5

B 7

C 8

D 9

MATHEMATICS

Use the place-value table below to answer question 15.

Hundred Thousands	Ten Thousands	Thousands	Hundreds	Tens	Ones
4	5	0	8	7	0
4	5	0	8	5	9

15. Which number has a value between the numbers shown in the table?

A   450,785

B   450,857

C   450,865

D   450,875

16. Divide:

$$1,528 \div 4$$

A   308

B   381

C   382

D   423

17. What are all the factors of 8?

A   1, 8

B   2, 4

C   2, 4, 8

D   1, 2, 4, 8

18. What is the standard form of one thousand two?

A   102

B   1,002

C   10,002

D   100,002

19. What symbol correctly compares the following numbers?

13,040 _____ 10,340

A   =

B   >

C   <

D   –

20. The county fair was held on Monday, Tuesday, and Wednesday.

> **A.** On Wednesday, 73,405 people came to the fair. Write the expanded form of the number of people who came to the fair on Wednesday.
>
> **B.** The total number of people who attended the fair on Monday was seventy-three thousand and forty-two. What is this number, written in standard form?
>
> **C.** On Tuesday, more people attended the fair than on Wednesday, and fewer people attended the fair than on Monday.
>
> How many people could have come to the fair on Tuesday? Explain how you know your answer is correct.

STOP

Lesson 2: Decimals

A **decimal** is a number that shows tenths, hundredths, and so on, by using a **decimal point**. In this lesson, you will write decimals in different forms. You will also compare and compute with decimals and money amounts.

Digits and Words

The number 3.25 has three digits: 3   .   2   5

In word form, 3.25 is written: three and twenty-five hundredths.

Drawings

Grids are often used to represent decimals in drawings.

The decimal 3.25 is represented by the shaded parts below.

TIP: In the word form of a decimal, the word "and" is spoken or written where the decimal point is located.

Eligible Content: M4.A.1.1.1, M4.A.1.1.2, M4.A.1.1.3

Place Value

Place-value tables show the value of the digits in a decimal.

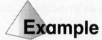 **Example**

This place-value table shows the decimal 3.25.

Hundreds	Tens	Ones	Decimal Point	Tenths	Hundredths
		3	.	2	5

Money

Money amounts are written as decimals. Even though money amounts are read as dollars and cents, the cents represent tenths and hundredths.

 **Example**

This place-value table shows the money amount $298.04.

	Hundreds	Tens	Ones	Decimal Point	Tenths	Hundredths
$	2	9	8	.	0	4

Because there are no tenths, a zero is written in the tenths place.

Practice

Directions: For Numbers 1 and 2, shade in the correct number of parts to show the decimals.

1. 0.70

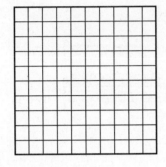

2. 1.09

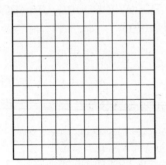

3. What decimal is shown by the shaded parts in the grid? _____

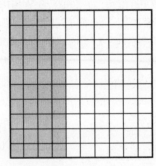

4. Make a drawing that shows the decimal 0.3.

Eligible Content: M4.A.1.1.1, M4.A.1.1.2, M4.A.1.1.3

5. How is 22.8 written in word form?

_____

6. How is 16.2 written in word form?

_____

7. Write a decimal with 7 in the tens place, 8 in the ones place, and 1 in the tenths place.

   _____

   How is this decimal written in word form?

_____

8. Write the money amount $905.21 in the following place-value table.

	Hundreds	Tens	Ones	Decimal Point	Tenths	Hundredths
$				•		

9. Write a money amount with 6 in the hundreds place, 2 in the tens place, 8 in the ones place, 4 in the tenths place, and 3 in the hundredths place.

   _____

10. In the number 53.72, what digit is in the hundredths place?

   A. 2

   B. 3

   C. 5

   D. 7

11. What is the standard form of ten and five tenths?

   A. 1.05

   B. 10.05

   C. 10.15

   D. 10.5

Eligible Content: M4.A.1.2.1

Number Lines

You can use a number line to show decimals. A number line with decimals will often show a whole number such as 1.

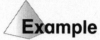 **Example**

What decimal should replace the *x* on the following number line?

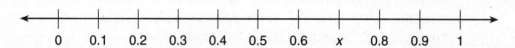

| 0 | 0.1 | 0.2 | 0.3 | 0.4 | 0.5 | 0.6 | *x* | 0.8 | 0.9 | 1 |

The decimals on the number line increase by .01 each time. The *x* is between 0.6 and 0.8.

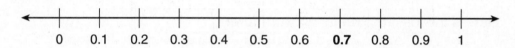

| 0 | 0.1 | 0.2 | 0.3 | 0.4 | 0.5 | 0.6 | **0.7** | 0.8 | 0.9 | 1 |

The decimal that should replace the *x* on the number line is 0.7.

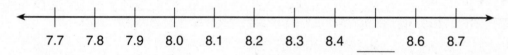 **Practice**

Directions: Use the number line to answer Numbers 1 through 3.

| 7.7 | 7.8 | 7.9 | 8.0 | 8.1 | 8.2 | 8.3 | 8.4 | ___ | 8.6 | 8.7 |

1. Write in the missing decimal on the blank under the number line.

2. What do the decimals increase by on the number line?

   A. 10

   B. 1

   C. 0.1

   D. 0.01

3. If one more decimal were added before 7.7 on the number line, what would it be?

   A. 6.6

   B. 6.8

   C. 7.6

   D. 7.8

Eligible Content: M4.A.1.2.2

Comparing Money Amounts

To compare decimals, compare the digits in each place-value position from left to right and look for digits that are different. Comparing money amounts is the same as comparing decimals to the hundredths place with a dollar sign ($).

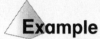 **Example**

Compare $58.92 and $58.96. The table shows the money amounts as decimals. They have the same digits in the tens, ones, and tenths place. The digits are different in the hundredths place.

Tens	Ones	Decimal Point	Tenths	Hundredths
5	8	•	9	2
5	8	•	9	6

In the hundredths place, the 2 is less than the 6.

Using words, you would say that $58.92 is less than $58.96.

Using symbols, you would write $58.92 < $58.96.

 **Example**

Order the following money amounts from **least** to **greatest**:

$6.70 $6.07 $7.17 $7.16

Compare the numbers.

6.70 > 6.07   6.70 < 7.17   6.70 < 7.16
6.07 < 7.17   6.07 < 7.16   7.17 > 7.16

Now write the amounts in order from least to greatest.

$6.07 $6.70 $7.16 $7.17

Practice

Directions: For Numbers 1 through 4, use $<$, $>$, or $=$ to compare the money amounts.

1. $82.36 _____ $82.52

3. $7.12 _____ $7.09

2. $12.40 _____ $12.40

4. $24.38 _____ $42.38

Directions: For Numbers 5 and 6, write the money amounts in order from **least** to **greatest**.

5. $6.55, $6.05, $6.50, $5.60 _____

6. $12.67, $11.67, $16.70, $12.76 _____

Directions: For Numbers 7 and 8, write the money amounts in order from **greatest** to **least**.

7. $35.84, $34.98, $34.61, $35.52 _____

8. $81.99, $82.35, $81.15, $82.15 _____

Directions: Use the following information to answer Numbers 9 and 10.

Four friends went out to lunch. Mike spent $4.10, Sarah spent $5.52, Abdul spent $4.19, and Sabina spent $5.38.

9. Which person spent the **most** money on lunch?

   A. Mike

   B. Sarah

   C. Abdul

   D. Sabina

10. Which person spent the **least** money on lunch?

   A. Mike

   B. Sarah

   C. Abdul

   D. Sabina

Eligible Content: M4.A.2.1.2, M4.A.3.2.1

Adding Decimals

Adding decimals is similar to adding whole numbers. You have to keep track of the place value of each digit. The decimal point will help you do this. Line up the digits with the same place values, as well as the decimal points. In the answer, move the decimal point down in the same place. Regroup where necessary.

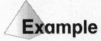 **Example**

Add: 4.58 + 3.11

Ones	•	Tenths	Hundredths
4	•	5	8
3	•	1	1
7	•	6	9

4.58 + 3.11 = 7.69

You can use pictures to help you understand how decimals are added.

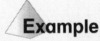 **Example**

Add: 0.73 + 0.46

Transfer the shaded squares from the grid representing 0.46 to the grid representing 0.73 until all squares have been transferred or until the first grid is full. If there are squares remaining, put them in a second grid.

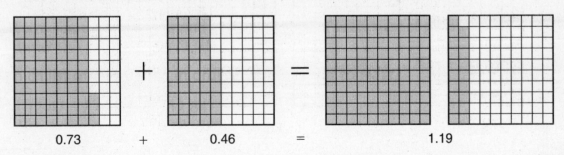

0.73   +   0.46   =   1.19

0.73 + 0.46 = 1.19

Practice

Directions: For Numbers 1 and 2, use the grids to show the sum. Then write the sum on the blank.

1.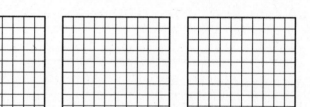

        1.32   +   1.89   =

_____

2.

        1.47   +   1.36   =

_____

Eligible Content: M4.A.2.1.2, M4.A.3.2.1

Directions: For Numbers 3 through 12, find the sum.

3. $4.61 + $8.09 = _____

4. 2.4 + 6.7 = _____

5. 12.5 + 0.2 = _____

6. 6.47 + 3.38 = _____

7. 120.72 + 0.15 = _____

8. 28.07 + 63.78 = _____

9. 67.1 + 8.7 = _____

10. $4.31 + $1.05 = _____

11. 9.06 + 103.78 = _____

12. 6.02 + 60.20 = _____

13. Alex paid $8.43 for a CD and $13.77 for a DVD. How much did he pay in all?

    _____

14. Monica was 3.9 feet tall last year. She has grown 0.4 feet since then. How tall is Monica now?

    _____

15. Will spent 3.50 hours on homework and 1.75 hours practicing the trombone. How much time did Will spend on homework and practicing the trombone altogether?

    _____

16. Reagan went to a movie. She paid $8.50 for her ticket and $6.95 for snacks. How much did Reagan pay in all?

    _____

17. At 9:00 in the morning, the temperature was 78.4°F. It rose 3.8 degrees before 3:00 in the afternoon. What was the temperature at 3:00?

    _____

Eligible Content: M4.A.2.1.2, M4.A.3.2.1

Subtracting Decimals

Subtracting decimals is similar to subtracting whole numbers. Line up the digits with the same place values, as well as the decimal points. In the answer, move the decimal point down in the same place. Borrow and regroup where necessary.

 Example

Subtract: 7.46 − 1.38

Ones	•	Tenths	Hundredths
7	•	$\cancel{4}^{3}$	$^{1}6$
1	•	3	8
6	•	0	8

Line up the ——— Borrow Regroup.
decimal points. a tenth.

7.46 − 1.38 = 6.08

You can also use pictures to help you understand how decimals are subtracted.

 Example

Subtract: 1.27 − 0.73

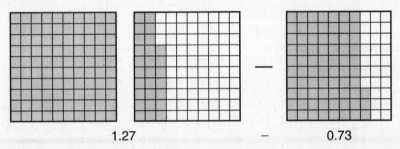

1.27   −   0.73

Cross out the number of squares that are in the second number from the first number.

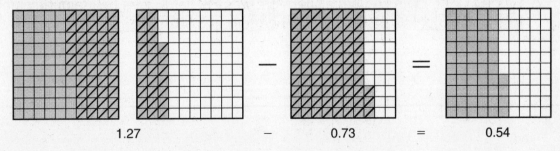

1.27   −   0.73   =   0.54

1.27 − 0.73 = 0.54

Practice

Directions: For Numbers 1 and 2, use the grids to show the difference. Then write the difference on the blank.

1. 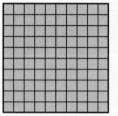 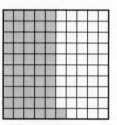 − 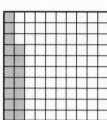 =

   1.17 − 0.51 =

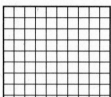 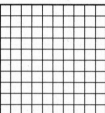 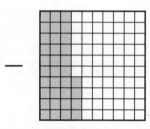

_____

2. 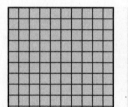 − 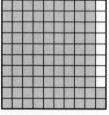 =

   1.92 − 0.34 =

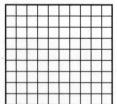 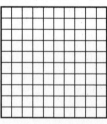 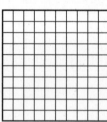

_____

Eligible Content: M4.A.2.1.2, M4.A.3.2.1

Directions: For Numbers 3 through 12, find the difference.

3. $9.57 − $4.24 = _____

4. 6.05 − 1.30 = _____

5. 19.25 − 0.49 = _____

6. 7.36 − 2.83 = _____

7. 114.08 − 9.72 = _____

8. 43.92 − 17.34 = _____

9. 91.40 − 6.52 = _____

10. $8.25 − $2.18 = _____

11. 6.24 − 0.83 = _____

12. 31.6 − 3.1 = _____

13. Miguel got $50.00 for his birthday. He spent $24.83 on a video game. How much money does Miguel have left?

_____

14. Reggie can run a mile in 9.33 minutes. Tyler can run a mile in 11.72 minutes. How much faster can Reggie run a mile than Tyler?

_____

15. Rodney's dog weighs 28.15 pounds. Kaitlyn's dog weighs 29.08 pounds. How much more does Kaitlyn's dog weigh than Rodney's dog?

_____

16. Madeline has $66.55 in her savings account. Veronica has $91.20 in her savings account. How much more money does Veronica have in her savings account than Madeline?

_____

17. On Saturday, Emily practiced the piano for 2.33 hours and played with friends for 4.25 hours. How much longer did Emily play with friends than practice the piano on Saturday?

_____

MATHEMATICS

1. What is three tenths written in standard form?

   A   0.03

   B   0.3

   C   3.10

   D   310

2. Which amount is greater than $41.53?

   A $41.35

   B $40.60

   C $41.60

   D $41.53

3. Subtract:

   $$6.29 - 4.83$$

   A   1.46

   B   1.66

   C   2.46

   D   2.66

4. Which statement is true?

   A $6.82 > $6.28

   B $5.07 > $5.70

   C $4.51 < $4.15

   D $3.68 > $3.82

5. Add:

   $$17.19 + 209.93$$

   A   217.12

   B   226.12

   C   227.02

   D   227.12

6. Which shows the word form of 2.9?

   A   two tenths and nine

   B   two and nine hundredths

   C   two and nine tenths

   D   twenty-nine tenths

7. Which letter is shown at 0.4 on the number line?

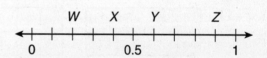

   A   W

   B   X

   C   Y

   D   Z

MATHEMATICS

8. Kat spent $12.95 on admission to the Philadelphia Zoo and $8.65 in the gift shop. How much did Kat spend at the Philadelphia Zoo?

    A $20.50

    B $20.60

    C $21.50

    D $21.60

9. Which shows 2.1 shaded?

    A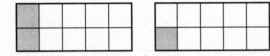

    B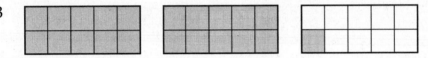

    C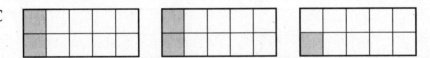

    D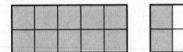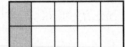

STOP

Eligible Content: M4.A.1.1.1, M4.A.1.1.2

Lesson 3: Fractions and Mixed Numbers

In this lesson, you will review fractions and mixed numbers. You will also add and subtract fractions.

Fractions

A **fraction** is a number that names parts of a whole or parts of a set. The **denominator** of the fraction is the bottom number. It tells you how many parts the whole is divided into or how many parts are in the set. The **numerator** of the fraction is the top number. It tells you how many parts of the whole or set you have.

$\frac{2}{5}$ ← **numerator**
   ← **denominator**

Parts of a Set

Fractions can show the number of parts of a set.

 **Example**

Charlotte has 4 balls.

What fraction of Charlotte's balls are footballs? $\frac{2}{4}$ (2 out of 4)

What fraction of Charlotte's balls are basketballs? $\frac{1}{4}$ (1 out of 4)

What fraction of Charlotte's balls are round? $\frac{2}{4}$ (2 out of 4)

Practice

Directions: Use the following figure to answer Numbers 1 and 2.

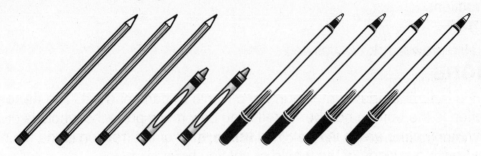

1. What fraction of the writing utensils are pencils? _____

2. What fraction of the writing utensils are crayons? _____

3. Lily has 7 T-shirts. Of those shirts, $\frac{2}{7}$ of them are gray, and $\frac{5}{7}$ of them are white. Draw Lily's t-shirts in the space below.

Directions: Use the following figure to answer Numbers 4 and 5.

4. What fraction of the fruit are oranges?

   A. $\frac{1}{8}$

   B. $\frac{3}{8}$

   C. $\frac{5}{8}$

   D. $\frac{6}{8}$

5. What fraction of the fruit are pineapples?

   A. $\frac{1}{8}$

   B. $\frac{3}{5}$

   C. $\frac{5}{8}$

   D. $\frac{8}{8}$

Parts of a Whole

Fractions can also show the number of parts of a whole.

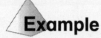 **Example**

Niki drew the figure below.

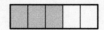

What fraction of the figure did Niki shade? $\frac{3}{5}$ (3 out of 5)

 **Practice**

Directions: Use the following information and figures to answer Numbers 1 through 4.

Mr. Harris asked his students to divide a square into equal parts and then shade some of the parts. This is how four students did it:

Jeff   Trisha   Mark   Traci

1. What fraction did Jeff shade? _____

2. What fraction did Trisha shade? _____

3. What fraction did Mark shade? _____

4. What fraction did Traci shade? _____

5. What fraction of the figure below is shaded? _____

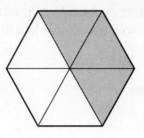

6. What fraction of the figure below is shaded? _____

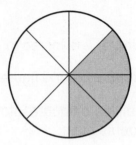

7. Shade some of the parts of the figure below. Then write a fraction that represents how much of the figure you shaded.

_____

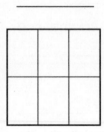

8. Draw a rectangle in the space below. Divide it into tenths. Then shade $\frac{6}{10}$ of the rectangle.

Eligible Content: M4.A.1.2.1

Number Lines

Fractions can be shown on a number line. Fractions shown on a number line can have any denominator. Watch to see how much the fractions on the number line increase each time.

**Example**

What fraction should replace the *x* on the number line?

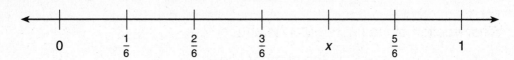

The fractions on the number line increase by $\frac{1}{6}$ each time. The *x* is between $\frac{3}{6}$ and $\frac{5}{6}$.

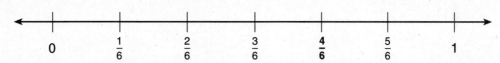

The fraction that should replace the *x* on the number line is $\frac{4}{6}$.

Example

Plot $\frac{1}{8}$, $\frac{2}{8}$, $\frac{4}{8}$, and $\frac{6}{8}$ on the number line.

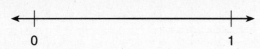

Divide the space between 0 and 1 into 8 equal sections. Each mark shows a fraction with a denominator of 8. The first mark shows where $\frac{1}{8}$ is, the second mark shows where $\frac{2}{8}$ is, and so on.

Practice

1. Plot $\frac{1}{5}$, $\frac{2}{5}$, $\frac{3}{5}$, and $\frac{4}{5}$ on the number line.

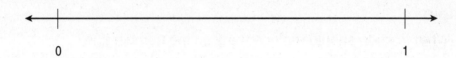

2. Plot $\frac{1}{10}$, $\frac{3}{10}$, $\frac{5}{10}$, and $\frac{9}{10}$ on the number line.

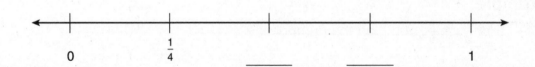

Directions: Use the following number line to answer Numbers 3 through 5.

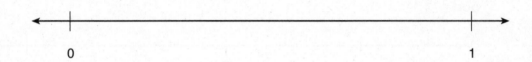

3. Write in the missing fractions on blanks under the number line.

4. By how much do the fractions increase on the number line?

   A. $\frac{1}{4}$

   B. $\frac{1}{2}$

   C. $\frac{2}{4}$

   D. $\frac{3}{4}$

5. What is another way to write the 1 on the number line?

   A. $\frac{1}{4}$

   B. $\frac{3}{4}$

   C. $\frac{4}{4}$

   D. $\frac{5}{4}$

Eligible Content: M4.A.3.2.2

Adding and Subtracting Fractions with Like Denominators

When fractions have the same denominators, they are said to have **like denominators**. To add or subtract fractions with like denominators, add or subtract the numerators and write the sum or difference over the denominator.

Example

Add: $\frac{2}{8} + \frac{3}{8}$

$$\frac{2}{8} \quad + \quad \frac{3}{8} \quad = \quad \frac{5}{8}$$

Example

Subtract: $\frac{4}{4} - \frac{3}{4}$

$$\frac{4}{4} \quad - \quad \frac{3}{4} \quad = \quad \frac{1}{4}$$

Examples

Add: $\frac{7}{10} + \frac{1}{10}$

$$\frac{7+1}{10} = \frac{8}{10}$$

$$\frac{7}{10} + \frac{1}{10} = \frac{8}{10}$$

Subtract: $\frac{4}{5} - \frac{1}{5}$

$$\frac{4-1}{5} = \frac{3}{5}$$

$$\frac{4}{5} - \frac{1}{5} = \frac{3}{5}$$

Practice

Directions: For Numbers 1 and 2, write the fraction for the shaded parts of each figure. Then find the sum or difference.

1.

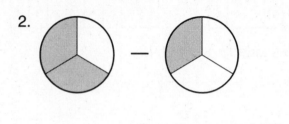

$+$

_____ $+$ _____ $=$ _____

2.

_____ $-$ _____ $=$ _____

3. Eric jogged for $\frac{1}{4}$ hour and biked for $\frac{2}{4}$ hour. How long did Eric jog and bike?

_____

4. Christina poured a cup of orange juice $\frac{4}{5}$ full and drank $\frac{2}{5}$ of the cup for breakfast. How much of the cup of orange juice is left?

_____

Directions: For Numbers 5 through 8, find the sum or difference.

5. $\frac{1}{10} + \frac{5}{10} =$ _____

6. $\frac{3}{7} + \frac{2}{7} =$ _____

7. $\frac{4}{6} - \frac{2}{6} =$ _____

8. $\frac{7}{9} - \frac{3}{9} =$ _____

Eligible Content: M4.A.1.1.1, M4.A.1.1.2

Mixed Numbers

A **mixed number** is a number that has a whole number part and a fractional part.

 Example

What mixed number represents the shaded parts of these figures?

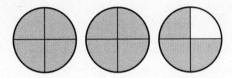

How many whole figures are shaded? 2

How many parts of the third figure are shaded? 3 out of 4

You write this as the fraction $\frac{3}{4}$.

The mixed number $2\frac{3}{4}$ represents the shaded parts of the figures.

Practice

Directions: Use the information and pies to answer Numbers 1 and 2.

The pictures show how much was left of 3 pies after a family picnic.

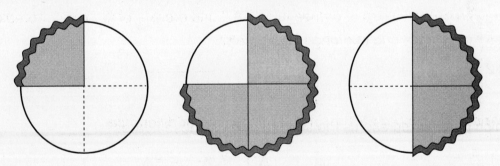

1. How many whole pies can be made with the pieces that are left? _____

2. Write a mixed number that tells how much pie is left altogether. _____

Directions: For Numbers 3 and 4, draw a picture for each mixed number.

3. $3\frac{1}{3}$

4. $1\frac{5}{10}$

5. Which number represents the shaded parts of these figures?

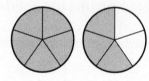

A. $1\frac{2}{5}$

B. $1\frac{3}{5}$

C. $2\frac{2}{5}$

D. $2\frac{3}{5}$

6. Which number represents the shaded parts of these figures?

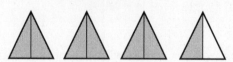

A. $3\frac{1}{2}$

B. $3\frac{2}{3}$

C. $4\frac{1}{3}$

D. $4\frac{1}{2}$

MATHEMATICS

1. Find the difference.

$$\frac{6}{7}$$
$$-\frac{3}{7}$$

A $\frac{9}{7}$

B $\frac{3}{7}$

C $\frac{1}{3}$

D $\frac{1}{4}$

2. Which equation is **true**?

A $\frac{2}{8} + \frac{3}{8} = \frac{5}{8}$

B $\frac{2}{4} + \frac{3}{4} = \frac{5}{8}$

C $\frac{2}{8} + \frac{3}{8} = \frac{5}{16}$

D $\frac{8}{8} - \frac{2}{8} = \frac{10}{16}$

3. At the carnival in Hershey, Jill saw 2 blue balloons, 3 red balloons, and 1 green balloon. What fraction of the balloons Jill saw were red?

A $\frac{1}{6}$

B $\frac{1}{3}$

C $\frac{3}{6}$

D $\frac{3}{3}$

4. C. J. spent $\frac{2}{6}$ of an hour studying. Which point shows how long C. J. studied?

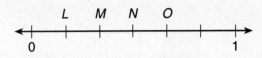

A L

B M

C N

D O

5. Find the sum.

$$\frac{4}{9}$$
$$+\frac{4}{9}$$

A $\frac{0}{9}$

B $\frac{1}{9}$

C $\frac{8}{9}$

D $\frac{8}{18}$

6. Which figures show $2\frac{1}{2}$ shaded?

A

B

C

D

7. Shawna shaded part of a figure, as shown below.

Which fraction shows how much of the figure Shawna shaded?

A $\frac{1}{4}$

B $\frac{1}{3}$

C $\frac{1}{2}$

D $\frac{3}{1}$

8. Robert shaded some circles, as shown below.

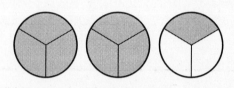

Which mixed number shows how many circles Robert shaded?

A $1\frac{5}{9}$

B $2\frac{1}{3}$

C $2\frac{2}{3}$

D $5\frac{1}{3}$

Use the number line below to answer question 9.

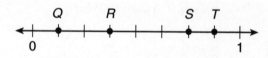

9. Which point shows $\frac{7}{8}$ on the number line?

A Q

B R

C S

D T

10. Carlos made the following number line.

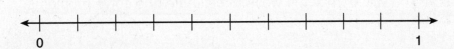

A. On the number line, put one point at $\frac{2}{10}$ and another point at $\frac{6}{10}$.

B. Solve: $\frac{6}{10} - \frac{2}{10}$.

C. By how much do the fractions increase on the number line? Explain how you got your answer.

STOP

Lesson 4: Estimation and Problem Solving

In this lesson, you will learn some ways to estimate and solve problems.

Estimation

Estimation tells you what number the answer to a problem is close to. You can use estimation before you solve the problem to be sure your answer is **reasonable** (makes sense).

Rounding Whole Numbers

Rounding is the most common way to estimate.

To round any whole number:

- Circle the digit to be rounded.

- Underline the number to the right of the digit to be rounded.

- Will the digit to be rounded stay the same or increase by 1?

  If the number underlined is **less than 5**, the digit to be rounded (circled number) **stays the same**.

  If the number underlined is **5 or greater**, the digit to be rounded (circled number) **increases by 1**.

- Write a zero or zeros as placeholders after the rounded digit.

Example

Round 2,349 to the nearest hundred.

The 3 is in the hundreds place, so circle it. The 4 is to the right of the 3, so underline it.

2 ,③4̲ 9

Because 4 is less than 5, the 3 stays the same. Write zeros as placeholders to the right of the 3.

Therefore, 2,349 rounded to the nearest hundred is 2,300.

Practice

1. Round 1,394 to the nearest ten. _____

2. Round 659 to the nearest hundred. _____

3. Round 143 to the nearest place value given.

   ten _____   hundred _____

4. Round 7,519 to the nearest place value given.

   hundred _____   thousand _____

5. Round 54,803 to the nearest place value given.

   ten _____   thousand _____

   hundred _____   ten thousand _____

6. Round 653,792 to the nearest place value given.

   hundred _____   ten thousand _____

   thousand _____   hundred thousand _____

7. What is 125,971 rounded to the nearest ten thousand?

   A. 120,000

   B. 126,000

   C. 130,000

   D. 136,000

8. What is 10,286 rounded to the nearest hundred?

   A. 10,000

   B. 10,200

   C. 10,290

   D. 10,300

Eligible Content: M4.A.3.1.2

Rounding Decimals

Rounding decimals is similar to rounding whole numbers.

To round any decimal:

- Circle the digit to be rounded.
- Underline the number to the right of the digit to be rounded.
- Will the digit to be rounded stay the same or increase by 1?

  If the number underlined is **less than 5**, the digit to be rounded (circled number) **stays the same**.

  If the number underlined is **5 or greater**, the digit to be rounded (circled number) **increases by 1**.

- Drop the digits to the right of the rounded digit (or change them to zeros).

 Example

Round 2.76 to the nearest tenth.

The 7 is in the tenths place, so circle it. The 6 is to the right of the 7, so underline it.

2 . ⑦6̲

Because 6 is greater than 5, the 7 increases by 1 to 8. Drop the digit to the right of the 8.

Therefore, 2.76 rounded to the nearest tenth is 2.8.

Rounding money amounts to the nearest dollar is the same as rounding decimals to the nearest whole number (or ones place).

 Example

Round $23.82 to the nearest dollar.

The 3 is in the ones place, so circle it. The 8 is in the tenths place, so underline it.

$2③. 8̲ 2

Because 8 is greater than 5, the 3 increases by 1 to 4. Instead of dropping the digits to the right of the 4, change them to zeros.

Therefore, $23.82 rounded to the nearest dollar is $24.00.

Eligible Content: M4.A.3.1.2

Practice

1. Round 3.43 to the nearest place value given.

   tenth _____   whole number _____

2. Round 5.72 to the nearest place value given.

   tenth _____   whole number _____

3. Round 4.96 to the nearest place value given.

   tenth _____   whole number _____

4. Round 3.89 to the nearest place value given.

   tenth _____   whole number _____

5. Round $23.45 to the nearest dollar. _____

6. Round $82.30 to the nearest dollar. _____

7. Round $83.93 to the nearest dollar. _____

8. Round $3.68 to the nearest dollar. _____

9. What is $9.50 rounded to the nearest dollar?

   A. $8.00

   B. $9.00

   C. $10.00

   D. $11.00

10. What is $23.39 rounded to the nearest dollar?

   A. $22.00

   B. $23.00

   C. $24.00

   D. $25.00

Eligible Content: M4.A.3.1.3

Rounding in Computation

You can use estimation when you compute. This will help you check your math to make sure your answer is reasonable. If the answer is not close to the estimated answer, go back and look for an error in the computation. You can also estimate when an exact answer is not necessary.

Round each of the numbers in the math problem. The place value you round to will depend on what numbers are in the problem.

Example

Estimate the sum of 345 and 487.

Step 1: **Round 345 to 300. Round 487 to 500.**

Step 2: **Add the rounded amounts.**

300 + 500 = 800

The estimated sum of 800 is close to the actual sum, 832.

Example

Estimate the product of 48 and 9.

Step 1: **Round 48 to 50. Round 9 to 10.**

Step 2: **Multiply the rounded amounts.**

$50 \times 10 = 500$

The estimated product of 500 is close to the actual product, 432.

Eligible Content: M4.A.3.1.3

Practice

Directions: For Numbers 1 through 8, find the estimated sum, difference, or product. Then find the actual sum, difference, or product.

1. 765 + 1,276

   estimate _____

   actual _____

2. 23,467 − 10,876

   estimate _____

   actual _____

3. 52 × 7

   estimate _____

   actual _____

4. 134,899 − 56,786

   estimate _____

   actual _____

5. 4,551 + 4,006

   estimate _____

   actual _____

6. 89,709 − 31,299

   estimate _____

   actual _____

7. 167,980 + 4,328

   estimate _____

   actual _____

8. 9 × 41

   estimate _____

   actual _____

Problem Solving

You can use a step-by-step strategy for solving problems whether you're inside or outside of the classroom. The practice activity will take you through this strategy.

Practice

Mount Davis in Somerset County is 3,213 feet above sea level. Mount McKinley in Alaska is 20,320 feet above sea level. Mount Everest, the world's tallest mountain, is 29,035 feet above sea level. How much taller is Mount Everest than Mount McKinley and Mount Davis combined?

Step 1: **Understand the problem.**

    1. What is the question that needs to be answered?

       _____

    2. What information is given in the problem? _____

       _____

       _____

Step 2: **Decide what operation(s) are needed to solve the problem.**

    3. Circle the operation(s) that are needed to solve this problem.

         addition   subtraction   multiplication

Step 3: **Set up the equation(s).**

    4. height of _____ 1 height of

       _____ 5 combined height

    5. height of _____ 2 combined height 5 how much taller

Eligible Content: M4.A.2.1.1, M4.A.2.1.2

Step 4: **Estimate.** (Round the heights of each of the mountains to the nearest thousand feet.)

6. Mount Davis: 3,213 → _____

7. Mount McKinley: 20,320 → _____

8. Mount Everest: 29,035 → _____

Use the rounded estimates in the equations from Step 3.

9. _____ + _____ = _____

10. _____ − _____ = _____

11. Mount Everest is **about** _____ feet taller than Mount Davis and Mount McKinley combined.

Step 5: **Do the math with the given values and check your answer.**

12. _____ + _____ = _____

13. _____ − _____ = _____

Check your answer:

14. _____ + _____ = _____

15. _____ − _____ = _____

16. Mount Everest is _____ feet taller than Mount Davis and Mount McKinley combined.

17. Is your answer close to your estimate in Step 4? _____

18. An amusement park being built near Erie plans to use 8 trains to carry passengers around. Each train will hold 76 passengers. How many passengers can be carried at one time?

    The number of passengers that can be carried at one time will be _____.

19. Derek won a book of ride tickets in a drawing. He gave 26 tickets to Kim and kept 38 tickets for himself. How many tickets were in the book of ride tickets to start with?

    There were _____ ride tickets in the book to start with.

20. The students at an elementary school near Harrisburg volunteered to help clean up around the building. The first day, 45 students volunteered. The second day, 40 different students volunteered. How many students volunteered in all?

    There were _____ students who volunteered.

21. There were 171 students that signed up for the town basketball league in a suburb of Pittsburgh. Each team will have 9 players. Every student that signs up will be on a team. How many teams will there be in the league?

There will be _____ teams in the league.

22. A canoe instructor can teach 12 people at one time how to ride a canoe along the Allegheny River. One day, 8 of the classes were completely filled and 1 class had 9 people in it. How many people did the canoe instructor teach that day?

The canoe instructor taught _____ people that day.

23. The school play was performed each day from Monday through Wednesday. On Monday, 275 people saw the play. On Tuesday, 312 people saw the play. Attendance increased to 442 people on Wednesday. How many more people saw the play on Monday and Tuesday combined than on Wednesday?

There were _____ more people that saw the play on Monday and Tuesday combined than on Wednesday.

24. Wendy bought 2 pairs of shoes for $29.95 each (tax included). She also used a coupon that saved $15.75 off her entire purchase. What was the total cost of Wendy's purchase?

The total cost of Wendy's purchase was _____.

25. On a recent drive from Philadelphia to Pittsburgh, Jerry filled up his gas tank two times with 12.4 gallons of gasoline. He also filled the tank once with 8.9 gallons of gasoline. How many gallons of gasoline did Jerry use in all?

Jerry used _____ gallons of gasoline.

26. Evan wanted to give most of his baseball card collection to his children. He kept 35 cards out of his original collection of 295 cards for himself. He divided the remaining cards evenly among his four children. How many cards did each child receive?

Each child received _____ cards.

Eligible Content: M4.A.3.1.3

Knowing When to Estimate

When you solve a math problem, you often need to find the exact answer. However, sometimes it is enough to estimate the answer. There are clues that tell you when it is okay to estimate. One clue to look for is the word "about."

Example

The Ridiculous Rascals performed two concerts in Allentown. At the first show, there were 8,825 people. At the second show, there were 11,429 people. **About** how many more people were at the second show than at the first show?

Because of the word "about," you can make it into an estimation problem.

Figure out the problem you are trying to solve.

11,429 − 8,825

Round both numbers to the nearest thousand and solve the problem.

11,000 − 9,000 = 2,000

There were about 2,000 more people at the second show than at the first show.

Practice

1. According to the 2000 U.S. Census, Erie County had a population of 280,843. Butler County had a population of 174,083. **About** how many people lived in these two counties altogether in 2000?

_____

2. According to the 2000 U.S. Census, Pittsburgh had a population of 334,563, Scranton had a population of 76,415, and Lancaster had a population of 56,348. **About** how many more people lived in Pittsburgh than in Scranton and Lancaster combined?

_____

3. Kyle earns $14.75 each hour he works at a landscaping company. **About** how much does Kyle earn in an 8-hour day?

_____

4. Jenna had lunch at The Sandwich Shack. She paid $3.25 for a sandwich, $1.80 for a cup of soup, and $1.19 for a drink. **About** how much did Jenna spend for lunch?

_____

5. The Susquehanna River basin covers 20,960 square miles of Pennsylvania land area. The Ohio River basin covers 15,614 square miles of Pennsylvania land area. **About** how many more square miles of Pennsylvania land area does the Susquehanna River basin cover than the Ohio River basin?

_____

People in Math

The year is 1770. The place is Virginia.
Two young men are talking with a very old man.
They've heard that the old man has a gift for math.

Thomas Fuller
(1710–1790)

They ask him, "How many seconds are in a year and a half?" The old man does the math in his head. In two minutes he tells them, "47,304,000 seconds." The two men use a pen and paper to check his answer. It's right! Then they ask, "How many seconds old is someone who has lived for 70 years, 17 days, and 12 hours?" The old man quickly says, "2,210,500,800 seconds." The two men check his answer, but this time they get a different number. The old man points out that they forgot to include the extra seconds from the leap years.

The old man was Thomas Fuller. Historians don't know much about his life. He was born in Africa. When he was 14, a terrible thing happened. He was sold to slave traders. Then he was taken to a plantation in Virginia. Fuller could not read or write. But he could do math in his head faster than most people could do it on paper. He became known as the "Virginia calculator" for his skill in math.

How did Fuller develop his amazing gift? No one knows for sure. But in the 1700s, Europeans brought back tales of African traders who were very good at doing math in their heads. The Africans' methods made them better mathematicians and businessmen than many of the Europeans.

MATHEMATICS

1. Which number rounded to the nearest thousand is 40,000?

   A 38,264

   B 39,821

   C 40,673

   D 42,009

2. Monica sold 8 bags of cookies. If each bag held 48 cookies, **about** how many cookies did Monica sell?

   A 50

   B 60

   C 300

   D 400

3. The table below shows how many people attended the school play.

   School Play

Day	Number of People
Friday	87
Saturday	92
Sunday	94

   About how many people attended the school play altogether?

   A 200

   B 240

   C 270

   D 290

4. Mr. Alston's class had 24 students. Mrs. Forman's class had 21 students. The classes combined and formed groups of 3 students. How many groups did they form?

   A 15

   B 45

   C 48

   D 135

5. Mr. Vollstedt started the school year with 2 boxes of markers. Each box held 20 markers. He has used 18 markers. How many markers does Mr. Vollstedt have left?

   A 25

   B 22

   C 20

   D 15

6. A bag contains these beads: 26 blue, 24 red, 19 yellow, and 22 green. **About** how many beads are in the bag?

   A 80

   B 90

   C 100

   D 110

7. Marty had 100 tickets for rides at an amusement park. He used 65 of the tickets. How many tickets does he have left?

   A 35

   B 45

   C 65

   D 165

8. Which estimate is **closest** to $13.99 × 3?

   A $ 4.20

   B $ 17.00

   C $ 42.00

   D $170.00

9. The fourth grade has 8 classes, and the third grade has 7 classes. Five students from each class went on a field trip. How many students went on the field trip altogether?

   A 20

   B 56

   C 75

   D 100

10. What is $72.83 rounded to the nearest dollar?

    A $72.00

    B $72.80

    C $72.90

    D $73.00

11. What number when rounded to the nearest ten is 160?

    A 155

    B 165

    C 167

    D 169

12. Which estimate is **closest** to 13,290 + 14,008?

    A 1,000

    B 2,700

    C 27,000

    D 32,000

13. What is 758,432 rounded to the nearest ten thousand?

    A 750,000

    B 758,430

    C 758,000

    D 760,000

MATHEMATICS

14. At Pedro's Pizza, a small pizza costs $9.85, and a large pizza costs $12.35. How much **more** does it cost to buy 2 large pizzas than 2 small pizzas?

A. Estimate the answer. Show all your work.

B. Find the exact answer. Explain how you found your answer.

STOP

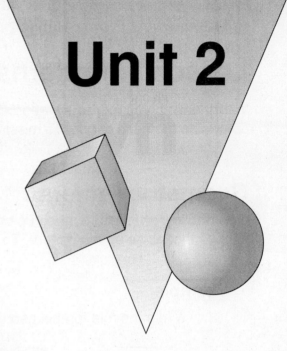

Unit 2

Algebraic Concepts

Patterns are almost everywhere you look. Think about
the tiles that make up your kitchen floors or the polka
dots on your favorite shirt. You can usually describe a
pattern by using a rule to get to the next shape or
number.

In this unit, you will find the missing shape or number in
a pattern and write the rule for the pattern. You will also
use symbols to represent missing numbers and
determine the values of these missing numbers.

In This Unit

Patterns and Functions

Algebra

Lesson 5: Patterns and Functions

In this lesson, you will review geometric patterns and number patterns. You will also determine the rules of and the missing elements in tables.

Geometric Patterns

Geometric patterns are made up of shapes. A geometric pattern usually repeats the shapes that make up the pattern. To describe a pattern is to write a **rule** for the pattern.

 Example

Write the rule for this geometric pattern and generate a similar pattern.

There is one square, followed by one star, followed by two circles. After the two circles, there is again one square, then one star, then two circles. The rule is square, star, two circles, square, and so on.

You can make a new pattern that is based on the rule of another pattern.

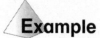 **Example**

The following pattern is based on the rule of the pattern in the first example.

There is one triangle, followed by one diamond, followed by two rectangles. After the two rectangles, there is again one triangle, then one diamond, then two rectangles. The new pattern follows a rule similar to that used in the first pattern, but the new pattern uses different shapes.

Eligible Content: M4.D.1.1.1, M4.D.1.1.2, M4.D.1.1.3

Use the Rule to Find the Next Figure

These three guidelines will help you find what figure comes next in a geometric pattern.

- Look at the shapes of the figures.

The pattern is circle, triangle, square, circle, triangle, square, circle, triangle, square.

The next figure in the pattern is a **circle**.

- Look at the sizes of the figures.

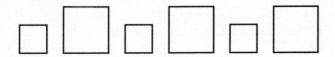

The pattern is small square, big square, small square, big square, small square, big square.

The next figure in the pattern is a **small square**.

- Look at the shading or marks in the figures.

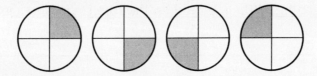

This pattern has different sections of the circle shaded: top right, bottom right, bottom left, top left.

The section that will be shaded next is the **top right section**.

 TIP: Sometimes a pattern will have figures with different shapes, sizes, and shadings or markings. You will need all three guidelines to find the next figure in the pattern.

Practice

Directions: For Numbers 1 and 2, draw the next three figures for each pattern. Then write the rule for the pattern.

1.   _____ _____ _____

   What is the rule for the pattern? _____

   _____

   _____

2. T ⊣ ⊥ ⊢ T _____ _____ _____

   What is the rule for the pattern? _____

   _____

   _____

3. Create your own geometric pattern using stars and moons)).

   Show three repetitions of the pattern.

   What is the rule for the pattern? _____

   _____

   _____

Eligible Content: M4.D.1.1.1, M4.D.1.1.2, M4.D.1.1.3

4. Draw the next three figures in the pattern.

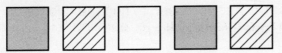 _____ _____ _____

What is the rule for the pattern? _____

_____

_____

Create a similar pattern in the space below.

5. Freda's parents are tiling their kitchen floor. They are following a pattern as they lay down the tiles. Draw in the next 5 rows of tiles to continue the pattern of the tiles.

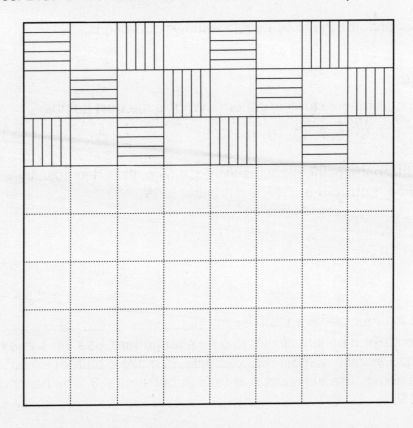

Eligible Content: M4.D.1.1.1, M4.D.1.1.2, M4.D.1.1.3

Number Patterns

There are many different kinds of **number patterns**. You need to find the rule for a pattern to find the next number or missing number in the pattern.

 **Example**

What is the rule for the pattern? What is the missing number?

2, 4, 6, _____, 10, 12

Because the numbers are increasing by 2, the rule is **add 2**. The missing number in the pattern is **8**.

 **Example**

What is the rule for the pattern? What is the missing number?

3; 18; _____; 648; 3,888

The numbers in this pattern are increasing rapidly. This means it is probably a multiplication pattern. The rule is **multiply by 6**. The missing number in the pattern is **108**.

Some number patterns may have a rule with two operations.

 **Example**

What is the rule for this pattern? What is the next number?

1, 7, 4, 10, 7, 13, 10, 16, 13, . . .

In this pattern, the numbers increase by 6, then decrease by 3. The rule is **add 6**, **subtract 3**. The next number is 19.

 TIP: To make a pattern similar to a number pattern, use the same rule, except use a different starting number. For example, to make a pattern similar to the first pattern above, use the same rule (add 2) but start at 3. The new pattern will be 3, 5, 7, 9, . . .

Eligible Content: M4.D.1.1.1, M4.D.1.1.2, M4.D.1.1.3

 **Practice**

Directions: For Numbers 1 through 4, use the number pattern to answer the questions.

1. 1, 3, 2, 4, 3, 5, 4, . . .

   What is the rule for the pattern? _____

   What are the next four numbers in the pattern? _____

2. 2, 1, 3, 2, 6, 5, 15, . . .

   What is the rule for the pattern? _____

   What are the next four numbers in the pattern? _____

3. 5, 14, 10, 19, 15, 24, 20, . . .

   What is the rule for the pattern? _____

   What are the next four numbers in the pattern? _____

4. Create your own pattern with two operations. Show at least 6 numbers in your pattern.

   _____

   What is the rule for the pattern? _____

5. What is the next number in this pattern?

   5, 10, 20, 25, 50, 55, 110, . . .

   A. 115
   B. 120
   C. 220
   D. 225

6. Which pattern follows the rule +2, ×3?

   A. 2, 4, 7, 14, 17, 34, 37, . . .
   B. 4, 6, 18, 20, 60, 62, 186, . . .
   C. 6, 8, 11, 13, 16, 18, 21, . . .
   D. 8, 16, 19, 38, 41, 84, 87, . . .

Input/Output Boxes

You can use any rule to change a number into a different number. One way to do this is to use an **input/output box**.

Example

Mr. Alvarez made an input/output box that uses a rule to change a number into a different number. He put three numbers through the box. What rule did Mr. Alvarez use to make his box?

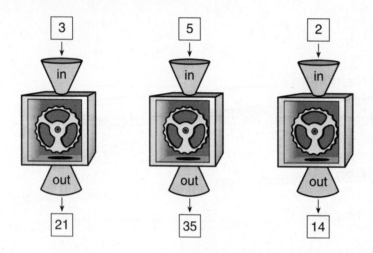

Look at each box. What happens to the input number inside the box to turn it into the output number?

$$3 \times 7 = 21 \qquad 5 \times 7 = 35 \qquad 2 \times 7 = 14$$

The rule for Mr. Alvarez's input/output box is ×7.

Practice

Directions: Use Mr. Alvarez's input/output box from the example above to answer Numbers 1 and 2.

1. Maria chose 13 as her input number. What was the output number?

2. Daniel chose 9 as his input number. What was the output number?

Eligible Content: M4.D.1.2.1, M4.D.1.2.2

Directions: Use the input/output boxes below to answer Numbers 3 through 5.

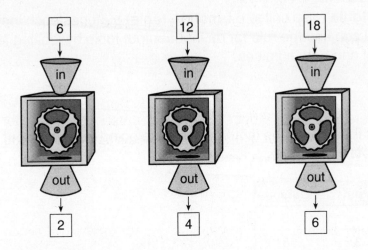

3. What is the rule for this set of boxes? _____

4. What will you get out of the box if 21 goes in? _____

5. What was the input number if the output number is 3? _____

Directions: Use the input/output boxes below to answer Numbers 6 and 7.

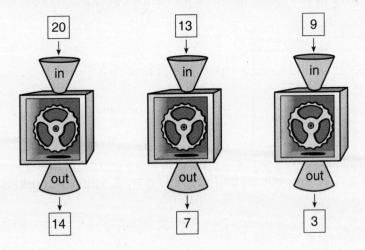

6. What is the rule for this set of boxes? _____

7. What is the output number when the input number is 14? _____

Input/Output Tables

An **input/output table** (also called a **function table**) matches each input value to its output value. You can find the rule for an input/output table by looking for the pattern between the input and output values.

Example

What is the rule for the input/output table going from the input column to the output column?

Input	Output
1	6
3	8
5	10
7	12

Each number in the output column is 5 more than the number in the input column. The rule going from the input column to the output column is +5.

Example

The input/output table shows the rule: multiply the input number by 2 and then add 3. What is the missing value in the input/output table?

Input	Output
2	7
4	11
6	
8	19

To find the missing value, first multiply 6 by 2, and then add 3 to the product.

$6 \times 2 = 12$

$12 + 3 = 15$

The missing value in the input/output table is 15.

Eligible Content: M4.D.1.2.1, M4.D.1.2.2

Practice

Directions: For Numbers 1 through 4, find the rule for going from the input column to the output column.

Directions: For Numbers 5 through 8, find the missing value in the input/output table.

1.

Input	Output
20	11
18	9
15	6
11	2

_____

5.

Input	Output
1	7
4	28
7	49
11	

_____

2.

Input	Output
2	31
5	34
6	35
9	38

_____

6.

Input	Output
3	15
4	16
7	19
9	

_____

3.

Input	Output
11	9
7	5
4	2
2	0

_____

7.

Input	Output
99	49
87	37
74	
68	18

_____

4.

Input	Output
1	4
3	14
4	19
6	29

_____

8.

Input	Output
2	5
5	
7	20
8	23

_____

MATHEMATICS

1. Lemont made the input/output table shown below.

Input	Output
1	3
3	9
4	12
6	18

What rule did Lemont use?

A   add 2

B   add 6

C   multiply by 3

D   multiply by 6

2. This input/output table shows the rule: multiply the input number by 4 and then subtract 4.

Input	Output
3	8
6	20
9	32
12	
16	

What 2 output numbers are missing in the table?

A   44, 60

B   48, 64

C   80, 76

D   80, 320

3. The numbers below follow a pattern.

16, 23, 30, 37, _____, 51

What is the missing number in the pattern?

A   39

B   44

C   49

D   54

4. Esther wrote numbers to form a number pattern, as shown below.

3, 6, 12, 24, __?__

What should be the next number in the pattern?

A   28

B   36

C   42

D   48

5. Which pattern has a rule of subtract 9 and then multiply by 2?

A   36, 27, 29, 20, 22, 13, 15

B   27, 36, 72, 81, 162, 169, 338

C   18, 9, 18, 9, 18, 9, 18

D   9, 18, 16, 25, 23, 31, 29

MATHEMATICS

Use the pattern below to answer question 6.

11, 15, 13, 17, 15, 19, 17

6. Which rule describes this pattern?

   A   add 4

   B   subtract 2

   C   add 2 then subtract 4

   D   add 4 then subtract 2

7. Dave created a pattern using shapes as shown below.

   Which pattern follows the same rule?

   A   W X Y Y W X Y Y W X Y Y

   B   W X X Y W X X Y W X X Y

   C   W W X Y W W X Y W W X Y

   D   W X Y Y X W X Y Y X W X Y Y

8. Miss Nelson's fourth graders put the following pattern on their bulletin board.

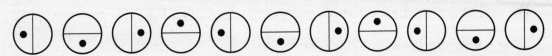

   What figure comes next in the pattern?

   A

   B

   C

   D

MATHEMATICS

9. Nora is making a bracelet with the following pattern.

□ ○ ▽ ▽ □ ○ ▽ ▽ □ ○ ▽ ▽ □ ○ ▽

A. Draw the next figure in the pattern.

B. Describe the rule for the pattern.

C. Nora wrote the pattern of numbers below.

6, 10, 14, 18, _?_, _?_, 30

The pattern continues. What are the 2 missing numbers?

D. What is the rule for Nora's number pattern from Part C?

STOP

Eligible Content: M4.D.2.1.1

Lesson 6: Algebra

In this lesson, you will match expressions and equations to problem situations. You will also review how to find a missing number or operation symbol in an equation or an inequality.

Expressions

An **expression** is a mathematical relationship between numbers and symbols. An expression is a number by itself or a number written using an operation sign such as $+$, $-$, $\times$, or $\div$. An expression does **not** have an equal sign or an inequality sign.

Examples

"Eight multiplied by nine" can be expressed as 8×9.

"Five fewer than seven" can be expressed as $7 - 5$.

"Ten more than six" can be expressed as $6 + 10$.

Equations

An **equation** is a mathematical sentence stating two expressions are equal. An equation uses an equal sign ($=$) to join the two expressions.

Examples

"Four multiplied by nine equals 36" can be expressed as $4 \times 9 = 36$.

"Nine subtracted from 15 equals six" can be expressed as $15 - 9 = 6$.

"Seven more than 22 equals 29" can be expressed as $22 + 7 = 29$.

Eligible Content: M4.D.2.1.1

Writing Expressions and Equations

You can write an expression or an equation to show the relationships in a story problem.

 Example

Cory biked 7 miles. He then took a short rest. After the rest, he biked 6 more miles to Lena's home. Write an expression that can help you find how many miles Cory biked.

miles biked before rest → 7 + 6 ← **miles biked after rest**

Example

Corinne planted 7 rows of flowers, and each row had 11 flowers. She planted a total of 77 flowers. Write an equation showing how many flowers Corinne planted.

number of rows → 7 × 11 = 77 ← **total number of flowers planted**

↑

number of flowers in each row

Some story problems have more facts than you need to write an expression or equation. Read the problem carefully to figure out what facts you need and what facts you can ignore when writing an expression or equation.

Example

Jackie made 200 donuts in 5 hours. She put the donuts in boxes that each held 10 donuts. Write an expression that can help you find how many boxes Jackie used.

The problem asks you to write an expression that can help you find how many boxes Jackie used. It does not ask how long it took to make the donuts. Therefore, your expression needs just two facts: Jackie made 200 donuts, and she stored them in boxes that each held 10 donuts.

number of donuts made → 200 ÷ 10 ← **number of donuts in each box**

If you solve the expression, you will find that Jackie used 20 boxes to hold 200 donuts.

Eligible Content: M4.D.2.1.1

Practice

Directions: For Numbers 1 through 5, write an expression to show the relationship given.

1. Thirty-two plus five _____

2. Nine times twenty-seven _____

3. Four more than fifteen _____

4. Seven less than sixty-four _____

5. Four minus two _____

Directions: For Numbers 6 and 7, write an expression to show the relationship given in the story.

6. Jonathan read 6 books in the series *Power of Greystoke* last month. Each book was 114 pages long. Write an expression that could help you find how many total pages Jonathan read.

7. Paige used 2 cups of flour to make 27 cookies. She took the cookies to school and gave one to each of the 22 students in her class. Write an expression that could help you find how many cookies Paige has left.

8. Haley is 16 years old. Haley's brother is 7 years younger than Haley. Which expression shows how to find the age of Haley's brother?

   A. $16 + 7$

   B. $16 - 7$

   C. 16×7

   D. $16 \div 7$

9. Frank worked 2 hours to earn $12. Then he worked 1 hour to earn $6 more. Which expression shows how to find how much money Frank has?

   A. $12 + 2$

   B. 12×6

   C. $6 + 12$

   D. 6×2

Directions: For Numbers 10 through 14, write an equation to show the relationship given.

10. Seven multiplied by six is equal to forty-two. _____

11. Thirty-nine subtracted from one hundred five is sixty-six. _____

12. Fourteen more than fifty-seven is equal to seventy-one. _____

13. Eighty-one less than ninety-four is equal to thirteen. _____

14. Seventeen times eight is one hundred thirty-six. _____

Directions: For Numbers 15 and 16, write an equation to show the relationship given in the story.

15. Cynthia wrote 5 thank-you notes to her aunts. Each thank-you note took her 10 minutes to write. She spent a total of 50 minutes writing thank-you notes. Write an equation showing how much time Cynthia spent writing the thank-you notes.

16. Laramie bought 15 packs of basketball cards for $3 a pack. Each pack held 10 cards. Laramie spent $45 dollars in all. Write an equation showing how much Laramie spent on the packs of basketball cards.

17. Kate can run 1 mile in 9 minutes. She ran 5 miles in 45 minutes. Which equation shows how long it took Kate to run 5 miles?

    A. $45 + 5 = 50$

    B. $9 - 5 = 4$

    C. $45 - 5 = 40$

    D. $9 \times 5 = 45$

18. Paul bought 50 pounds of red bricks for $10. Each of the 25 red bricks that he bought weighed 2 pounds. Which equation shows how many pounds of bricks Paul bought?

    A. $2 \times 25 = 50$

    B. $10 + 25 = 35$

    C. $50 - 25 = 25$

    D. $50 - 10 = 40$

Eligible Content: M4.D.2.2.2

Number Sentences

A **number sentence** compares two or more expressions with each other. An equation is a number sentence that says two expressions are equal. An **inequality** is a number sentence that compares two unequal expressions with the symbols < (is less than) or > (is greater than).

Example

Find the missing symbol in the number sentence.

24 _____ 45 − 19

First, subtract 19 from 45. Then, put your answer into the original number sentence.

45 − 19 = 26

24 _____ 26

Now, ask yourself: What symbol makes this number sentence true? The missing symbol is a less than sign (<).

24 < 26

So, 24 < 45 − 19.

Sometimes it is not an =, <, or > symbol that is missing in a number sentence. You may be given a number sentence where the symbol missing is an operation sign (+, −, ×, or ÷).

Example

Find the missing symbol in the number sentence.

15 _____ 18 = 33

Adding 15 and 18 equals 33. The missing symbol is an addition sign.

15 + 18 = 33

Practice

Directions: For Numbers 1 through 10, write the missing symbol (=, <, or >) on the blank that makes the number sentence true.

1. $12 - 4$ _____ 9

2. $7 + 8$ _____ 15

3. 17 _____ 2×8

4. 3 _____ $9 \div 3$

5. $3 + 5$ _____ 10

6. $18 - 9$ _____ 8

7. 9 _____ $8 \div 2$

8. 7×9 _____ 64

9. $14 - 8$ _____ 6

10. 48 _____ 7×6

Directions: For Numbers 11 through 20, write the missing symbol (+, −, ×, or ÷) on the blank that makes the number sentence true.

11. 3 _____ $8 = 24$

12. 16 _____ $12 = 4$

13. 9 _____ $3 = 3$

14. 13 _____ $9 = 4$

15. $13 = 8$ _____ 5

16. $34 = 18$ _____ 16

17. 8 _____ $4 = 2$

18. $18 = 9$ _____ 2

19. 61 _____ $56 = 5$

20. 9 _____ $3 = 27$

Eligible Content: M4.D.2.2.1

Open Number Sentences

Sometimes you will see an equation with a missing number. The missing number may be represented by a ○, □, △, or ▽. Your job is to find the missing number that makes the equation true.

Example

What number replaces the □ in this equation?

$$6 + \square = 13$$

You need to find out what number added to 6 will equal 13.

$$6 + \mathbf{7} = 13$$

The number **7** replaces the □ in the equation.

Example

What number replaces the □ in this equation?

$$2 \times \square = 16$$

You need to find out what number multiplied by 2 will equal 16.

$$2 \times \mathbf{8} = 16$$

The number **8** replaces the □ in the equation.

Example

What number replaces the △ in this equation?

$$\triangle - 2 = 7$$

You need to find out what number you can subtract 2 from to equal 7.

$$\mathbf{9} - 2 = 7$$

The number **9** replaces the △ in the equation.

Practice

Directions: For Numbers 1 through 16, find the number that replaces each symbol.

1. $5 + \square = 8$ $\square = $ _____

2. $\bigcirc - 5 = 11$ $\bigcirc = $ _____

3. $\triangledown \times 6 = 24$ $\triangledown = $ _____

4. $14 - \square = 9$ $\square = $ _____

5. $\bigcirc + 3 = 12$ $\bigcirc = $ _____

6. $8 \times \triangledown = 56$ $\triangledown = $ _____

7. $20 \div \triangle = 5$ $\triangle = $ _____

9. $\square + 9 = 18$ $\square = $ _____

10. $25 - \bigcirc = 13$ $\bigcirc = $ _____

11. $\triangledown \times 3 = 21$ $\triangledown = $ _____

12. $16 \div \square = 4$ $\square = $ _____

13. $6 + \bigcirc = 15$ $\bigcirc = $ _____

14. $\triangledown \times 7 = 35$ $\triangledown = $ _____

15. $35 \div \square = 5$ $\square = $ _____

8. What number replaces the $\square$ in this equation?

$$13 + \square = 22$$

A. 9

B. 11

C. 13

D. 22

16. What number replaces $\bigcirc$ in this equation?

$$32 \div \bigcirc = 4$$

A. 4

B. 6

C. 8

D. 9

• • • • • • • • • • • • • • **PSSA Practice begins on the following page.**

MATHEMATICS

1. Last week, Hector worked 1 hour and picked 252 apples. This week, Hector worked 3 hours and picked 545 apples. Which shows how to find how many apples Hector picked?

   A   252 + 545

   B   545 − 252

   C   252 × 3

   D   545 × 3

2. Which pair of expressions is compared correctly?

   A   4 + 13 < 33 ÷ 3

   B   8 × 7 = 5 × 10

   C   48 − 3 > 3 × 15

   D   51 − 19 > 12 + 18

Use the number sentence below to answer question 3.

$$9 - 7 \ \square \ 16$$

3. Which symbol goes in the □ to make the number sentence true?

   A   =

   B   >

   C   <

   D   −

Use the equation below to answer question 4.

$$6 \times \square = 48$$

4. Which symbol goes in the □ to make the equation true?

   A   8

   B   12

   C   24

   D   42

Use the number sentence below to answer question 5.

$$15 \times 5 \ \square \ 75$$

5. Which symbol goes in the □ to make the number sentence true?

   A   =

   B   >

   C   <

   D   −

Use the equation below to answer question 6.

$$20 \ \square \ 4 = 16$$

6. Which symbol goes in the □ to make the equation true?

   A   +

   B   −

   C   ×

   D   ÷

MATHEMATICS

Use the number sentence below to answer question 7.

$$89 \square\ 37 + 52$$

7. Which symbol goes in the □ to make the number sentence true?

   A $<$

   B $>$

   C $=$

   D $-$

8. Kathryn has 2 bookcases with a total of 6 bookshelves between them. Each bookshelf has 18 books on it. Which shows how to find how many books Kathryn has?

   A $2 + 18$

   B $18 - 6$

   C 6×18

   D $18 + 6$

Use the equation below to answer question 9.

$$20 - \square = 12$$

9. What number should go in the □ to make this equation true?

   A   6

   B   8

   C   10

   D   12

10. Nathan charges $5.00 for each lawn that he mows. This weekend, he spent 2 hours mowing 4 lawns and earned $20.00. Which shows how much money Nathan earned?

   A $4 + 20 = 24$

   B $20 \times 4 = 80$

   C $20 - 5 = 15$

   D $4 \times 5 = 20$

Use the number sentence below to answer question 11.

$$59 \square\ 412 - 354$$

11. Which symbol goes in the □ to make the number sentence true?

   A $<$

   B $>$

   C $=$

   D $+$

Use the equation below to answer question 12.

$$\square \times 4 = 32$$

12. What number should go in the □ to make this equation true?

   A   4

   B   5

   C   7

   D   8

STOP

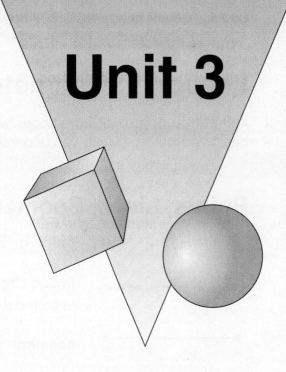

Unit 3

Geometry

Have you ever played in a tree house? Did you help build it? When you build a tree house you are using geometry. You are also using geometry skills when you make a kite or figure out the best way to get to the Philadelphia Zoo. From the invention of the wheel to the exploration of our planet, geometry has helped people understand and get around in our world.

In this unit, you will learn about the figures that are all around you. You will learn how to identify, classify, and compare different figures. You will also learn about symmetry and finding locations on a grid.

In This Unit

Geometric Figures

Geometric Concepts

Lesson 7: Geometric Figures

In this lesson, you will learn about two- and three-dimensional figures. Here is some basic vocabulary to help you understand such figures.

Points, Lines, Segments, and Angles

•
R

point: a single location or position (*R*)

line: a straight path that goes on forever in both directions ($\overleftrightarrow{AB}$ or *x*)

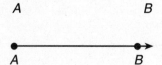

segment: part of a line with two endpoints ($\overline{AB}$)

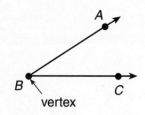

ray: part of a line that begins at one endpoint and goes on forever in one direction ($\overrightarrow{AB}$)

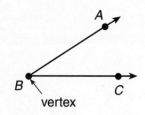

angle: formed by two rays with a common endpoint, called a vertex; measured in degrees (°) ($\angle ABC$, $\angle CBA$, or $\angle B$)

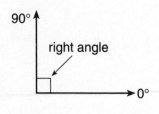

right angle: an angle that forms a square corner; measures exactly 90°

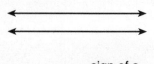

parallel lines: lines that are in the same plane (flat surface) and do not cross each other

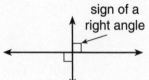

perpendicular lines: lines that cross each other and form right angles (square corners)

Eligible Content: M4.C.1.2.1, M4.C.1.2.2

Practice

Directions: For Numbers 1 and 2, label the type of lines that each real-world object represents (parallel or perpendicular).

1. highway

_____

2. railroad crossing sign

_____

3. Find two objects in your classroom and name the types of lines they model.

objects	lines
_____	_____
_____	_____

4. Write *parallel lines* or *perpendicular lines* on the blank under each drawing.

          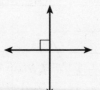

_____   _____

5. What is shown in the figure below?

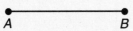

   A. point
   B. line
   C. line segment
   D. ray

6. What is shown in the figure below?

   A. point
   B. line
   C. line segment
   D. ray

Two-dimensional Figures

The chart below shows some common **two-dimensional figures**.

Circle	Triangle	Quadrilateral
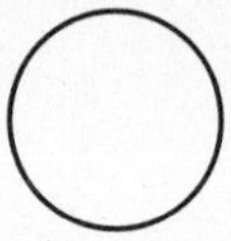 2-dimensional figure with 0 straight sides	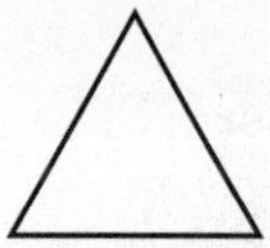 a polygon with 3 sides and angles	a polygon with 4 sides and angles
Pentagon	**Hexagon**	**Octagon**
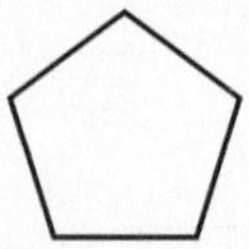 a polygon with 5 sides and angles	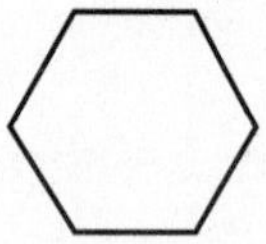 a polygon with 6 sides and angles	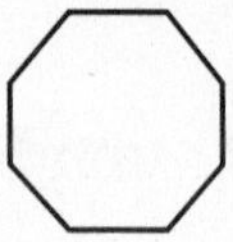 a polygon with 8 sides and angles

Polygons are two-dimensional figures with three or more straight sides. A circle is a two-dimensional figure, but it is **not** a polygon because it has no straight sides. Polygons with four sides and four angles are called **quadrilaterals**. The chart below shows six different quadrilaterals.

Parallelogram	Rhombus	Rectangle
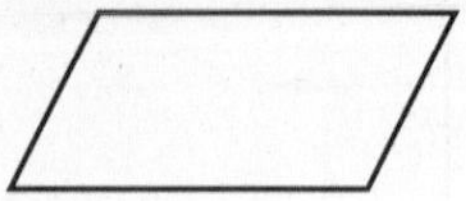 opposite sides are equal and parallel	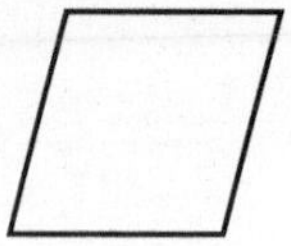 a parallelogram with 4 equal sides	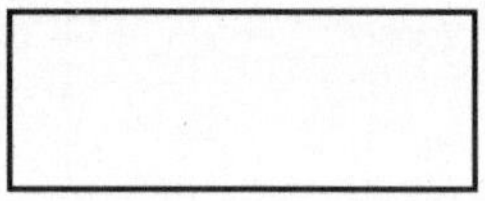 a parallelogram with 4 right angles
Square	**Trapezoid**	**Isosceles Trapezoid**
a parallelogram with 4 equal sides and 4 right angles	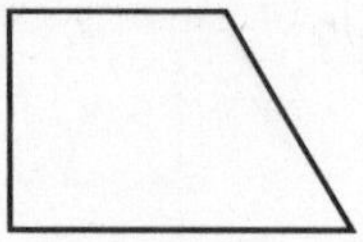 1 pair of parallel sides	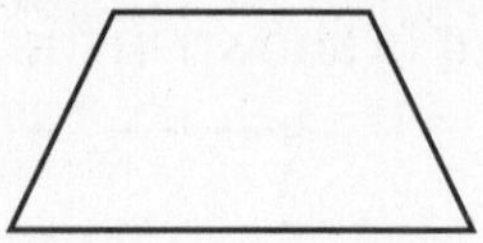 1 pair of parallel sides and 1 pair of equal sides

igible Content: M4.C.1.1.1

Practice

Directions: For Numbers 1 through 4, draw a figure for each description. Then write the name of the figure.

1. a polygon with 3 sides

figure _____

2. a parallelogram with 4 equal sides and 4 right angles

figure _____

3. a two-dimensional figure that is not a polygon

figure _____

4. a polygon with 6 sides

figure _____

5. Ann says the figure below is a rhombus, Sarah says it is a square, and Jen says it is a rectangle.

Who is correct? Explain your answer._____

_____

6. Under each real-world object, write the name of the polygon that it looks like.

_____   _____   _____

_____   _____   _____

7. Which quadrilateral does **not** have two sets of parallel sides?

   A. square

   B. rhombus

   C. trapezoid

   D. parallelogram

8. Which polygon is **not** a parallelogram?

   A. square

   B. triangle

   C. rhombus

   D. rectangle

Eligible Content: M4.C.1.1.2

Three-dimensional Figures

Three-dimensional figures have three dimensions: length, width, and height. Here are some examples of three-dimensional figures.

Shape	Solid
Rectangular Prism	
Cube	
Triangular Pyramid	
Rectangular Pyramid	
Sphere	

Faces, Edges, and Vertices

Some solid figures have faces, edges, and vertices. The **faces** of solid figures are two-dimensional figures. The segments formed where these faces meet are **edges**. Any point where edges meet is a **vertex**.

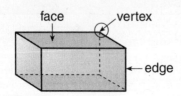

face   vertex

edge

Example

How many faces, edges, and vertices does a rectangular prism have?

First, count the faces. There are 2 short rectangular faces on the ends and 4 long rectangular faces. Altogether there are 6 faces.

Next count the edges. There are 12 edges.

Finally, count the vertices. Each corner is a vertex. There are 8 vertices.

So, a rectangular prism has 6 faces, 12 edges, and 8 vertices.

Practice

1. Under each real-world object, write the name of the solid figure that it looks like.

_____   _____

_____   _____

Eligible Content: M4.C.1.1.2

Directions: For Numbers 2 and 3, write a description of the object shown. Give the name of the solid figure, describe the shapes of the faces, and tell the number of faces, edges, and vertices.

2. 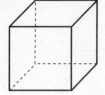 _____

_____

_____

3. 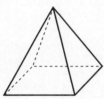 _____

_____

_____

4. Levi says that a cube is also a rectangular prism. Is he correct? Explain why or why not.

_____

_____

_____

5. Which solid has no flat surfaces? _____

6. Write down three objects in your classroom. Then, write the name of the three-dimensional figure that each object looks like.

_____

_____

_____

1. Which real-world object looks **most** like a cube?

   A

   B

   C

   D

Use the drawing below to answer question 2.

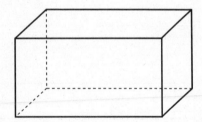

2. What three-dimensional shape is this object?

   A   rectangular prism

   B   pyramid

   C   cube

   D   rectangle

3. Which pair of lines is perpendicular?

   A

   B

   C

   D

Use the figure below to answer question 4.

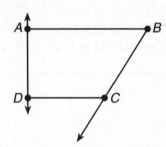

4. In this figure, which is a ray?

   A $\overline{AB}$

   B $\overrightarrow{BC}$

   C $\overline{CD}$

   D $\overleftrightarrow{AD}$

5. Which polygon has 5 sides?

   A   rhombus

   B   trapezoid

   C   pentagon

   D   hexagon

6. Use the following figures to answer Parts A through C.

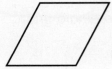

_____   _____

A. Write the names of each figure on the blanks.

B. Describe one way that the two figures are similar.

C. Describe one way that the two figures are different.

STOP

Lesson 8: Geometric Concepts

In this lesson, you will review symmetry and the coordinate grid.

Symmetry

A figure has **symmetry** when it can be folded so that its two halves match.

Examples

You can fold this pentagon along its **line of symmetry**. Both halves will match.

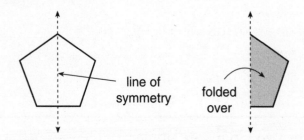

line of symmetry

folded over

Some figures have more than one line of symmetry. This rectangle can be folded two different ways so the halves match.

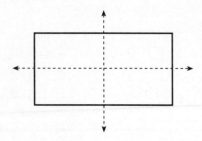

Some figures do not have any lines of symmetry. There are no places you can fold this figure so that both halves match.

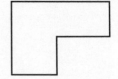

Eligible Content: M4.C.2.1.1

Practice

1. Half of this figure is missing. Draw and shade the matching half of the figure.

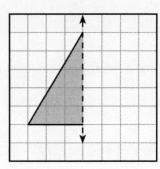

2. How many lines of symmetry does the following figure have? _____

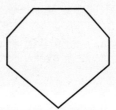

3. Circle the figure below that does **not** have a line of symmetry.

4. Draw the line(s) of symmetry on the figures.

5. Draw a figure that has no lines of symmetry.

6. Draw a figure that has two lines of symmetry.

7. Draw a figure that has one line of symmetry.

8. Which letter does **not** have a line of symmetry?

   A. **C**

   B. **Z**

   C. **W**

   D. **X**

9. Which letter has two lines of symmetry?

   A. **A**

   B. **D**

   C. **K**

   D. **X**

Eligible Content: M4.C.3.1.1

The Coordinate Grid

The coordinate grid has a **horizontal axis** (called the **x-axis**) and a **vertical axis** (called the **y-axis**). The x-axis and the y-axis meet at a point called the **origin**.

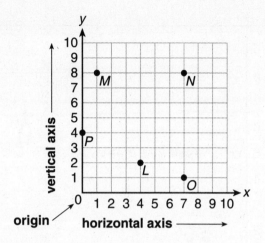

Locating Points

Points on the coordinate grid are described by **ordered pairs**. An ordered pair is made up of two numbers inside parentheses and separated by a comma, such as (4, 2).

The numbers inside an ordered pair are the **coordinates** of a point. The first number in an ordered pair tells you where to go on the x-axis. The second number tells you where to go on the y-axis. The origin is located at (0, 0).

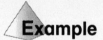

Example

What is the ordered pair for *L* on the coordinate grid above?

To get to *L*, start at the origin and go 4 units to the right along the x-axis. Then go 2 units up the y-axis.

The ordered pair for *L* is (4, 2).

Practice

Directions: Use the grid below to answer Numbers 1 through 6.

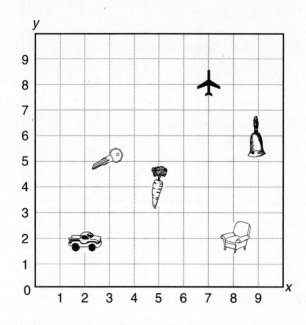

1. What ordered pair describes the location of the carrot? _____

2. What object is located at (2, 2)? _____

3. Draw a circle at (2, 7).

4. What object will you find if you move 1 unit left and 6 units up from the chair?

   _____

   What is the ordered pair for that object? _____

5. What ordered pair describes the location of the bell?

   A. (6, 8)

   B. (6, 9)

   C. (9, 6)

   D. (8, 9)

6. What object is located at (3, 5)?

   A. truck

   B. key

   C. carrot

   D. chair

Eligible Content: M4.C.3.1.1

Directions: Use the grid below to answer Numbers 7 through 12.

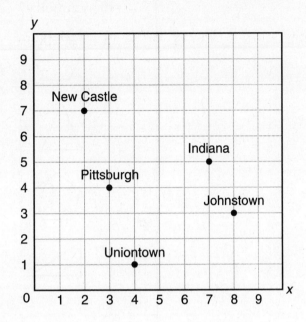

7. What ordered pair describes the location of Uniontown? _____

8. What city is located at (7, 5)? _____

9. Plot Punxsutawney at (8, 7).

10. What city will you find if you move 1 unit left and 3 units up from Pittsburgh?

   _____

   What is the ordered pair for that city? _____

11. What ordered pair describes the location of Johnstown?

   A. (8, 3)

   B. (3, 8)

   C. (0, 8)

   D. (8, 0)

12. What city is located at (3, 4)?

   A. New Castle

   B. Indiana

   C. Uniontown

   D. Pittsburgh

MATHEMATICS

1. Which figure has exactly one line of symmetry?

A

B

C

D

2. Which letter is found at (5, 4)?

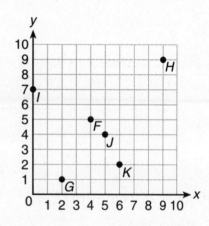

Use the grid below to answer question 2.

A   F

B   H

C   J

D   K

3. Which figure does **not** have any lines of symmetry?

A

B

C

D

Use the grid below to answer question 4.

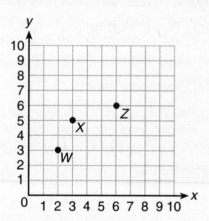

4. What is the location of point X?

A   (3, 5)

B   (5, 3)

C   (2, 3)

D   (3, 2)

STOP

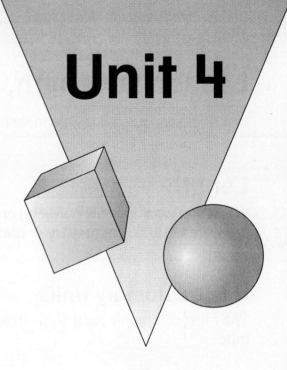

Unit 4

Measurement

Have you ever been in a swimming pool and wondered how deep the water was? Or how much water the pool could hold? These are just a couple examples of how measurement can be used in everyday life. You may not realize it, but every time you look at a clock for the time or stand on a scale to weigh yourself, you are measuring.

In this unit, you will learn about measurements such as length, weight, and capacity. You will also review telling time and learn how to find how much time has passed between events.

In This Unit

Length, Weight, and Capacity

Time

Eligible Content: M4.B.2.2.1

Lesson 9: Length, Weight, and Capacity

In this lesson, you will review measurements of length, weight, and capacity.

Length

When you want to know how long an object is, you measure its **length**. Length can be measured in **U.S. customary** or **metric units**.

U.S. Customary Units

The most commonly used U.S. customary units of length are **inch**, **foot**, **yard**, and **mile**.

1 inch (in.)

The diameter of a quarter is about 1 inch

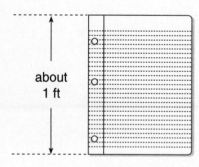

1 foot (ft) = 12 in.

The longer side of a sheet of notebook paper is about 1 foot.

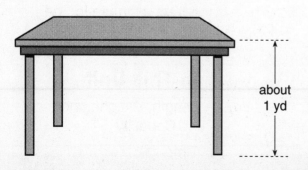

1 yard (yd) = 3 ft

The height of a kitchen table is about 1 yard.

Eligible Content: M4.B.2.2.1

1 mile (mi) = 1,760 yd
A person can walk 1 mile in about 20 minutes.

Practice

Directions: For Numbers 1 through 3, write an estimate for the length of each item using the unit given.

1. an envelope: _____ inches

2. a soccer field: _____ yards

3. a notebook: _____ inches

Directions: For Numbers 4 through 6, fill in the blank with the most reasonable U.S. customary unit of length.

4. An adult is about 6 _____ tall.

5. The ceiling is about 3 _____ tall.

6. A baby is about 20 _____ long.

7. Which is the **best** estimate for the distance a person might jog each day?

   A.   3 miles

   B.   30 miles

   C.   300 miles

   D. 3,000 miles

8. Which is the **best** estimate for the length of a stapler?

   A. 8 miles

   B. 8 yards

   C. 8 feet

   D. 8 inches

Using an Inch Ruler

An inch ruler is used to measure items that are 1 foot or less. A ruler is divided into inches. There are 12 inches in 1 foot. Most rulers are further divided into fractions of an inch.

**Example**

How long is this insect to the nearest $\frac{1}{4}$ inch?

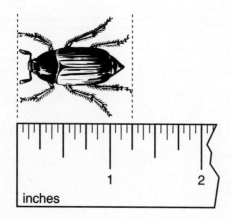

Step 1: **Align the left edge of the ruler with the left edge of the object that you are measuring.**

Step 2: **Count the number of full inches the object has and then the number of $\frac{1}{4}$ inches past the last full inch.**

The line is one $\frac{1}{4}$ mark after the 1 on the ruler. The length of the insect is $1\frac{1}{4}$ inches.

Eligible Content: M4.B.2.1.1

Practice

Directions: For Numbers 1 through 4, use an inch ruler to measure each object to the nearest $\frac{1}{4}$ inch.

1.

_____ inches

2.

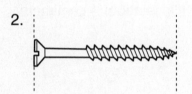

_____ inches

3.

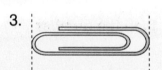

_____ inches

4.

_____ inches

Metric Units

The most commonly used metric units of length are **millimeter**, **centimeter**, **meter**, and **kilometer**.

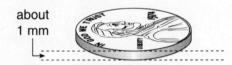

about
1 mm

1 millimeter (mm)

The thickness of a penny is about 1 millimeter.

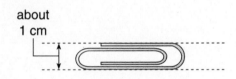

about
1 cm

1 centimeter (cm) = 10 mm

The width of a large paper clip is about 1 centimeter.

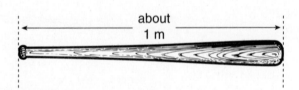

about
1 m

1 meter (m) = 100 cm

The length of a major league baseball bat is about 1 meter.

1 kilometer (km) = 1,000 m

Most people can walk 1 kilometer in about 8 minutes.

Eligible Content: M4.B.2.2.1

Practice

Directions: For Numbers 1 through 4, write an estimate for the length of each item using the unit given.

1. a piece of chalk: _____ centimeters

2. a wall in your classroom: _____ meters

3. distance across your town: _____ kilometers

4. a basketball court: _____ meters

Directions: For Numbers 5 through 8, fill in the blank with the most reasonable metric unit of length.

5. The distance from Harrisburg to Philadelphia is about 170 _____.

6. A license plate is about 30 _____ long.

7. A swimming pool is about 25 _____ long.

8. A fingernail is about 15 _____ wide.

9. Which is the **best** estimate for the length of a football field?

   A. 50 meters
   B. 75 meters
   C. 100 meters
   D. 125 meters

10. Which is the **best** estimate for the width of a postage stamp?

   A. 2 centimeters
   B. 2 meters
   C. 2 kilometers
   D. 2 millimeters

Eligible Content: M4.B.2.1.1

Using a Centimeter Ruler

A centimeter ruler is used to measure items that are 30 centimeters or less. A ruler is divided into centimeters. There are 10 millimeters in 1 centimeter.

 Example

How long is this pen to the nearest centimeter?

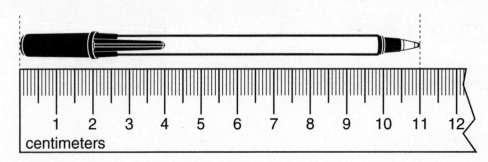

Step 1: **Align the left edge of the ruler with the left edge of the object that you are measuring.**

Step 2: **Count the number of full centimeters.**

The end of the pen lines up with the 11 on the ruler. The length of the pen is 11 centimeters.

TIP: Some rulers measure both inches and centimeters. These rulers have inches on one side and centimeters on the other side.

Eligible Content: M4.B.2.1.1

Practice

Directions: For Numbers 1 through 4, use a centimeter ruler to measure each object to the nearest centimeter.

1.

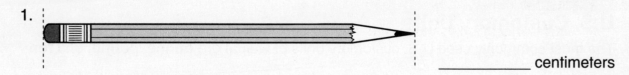

_____ centimeters

2.

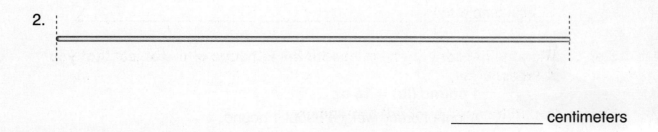

_____ centimeters

3.

CHOOSY FRUIT
GUM

_____ centimeters

4.

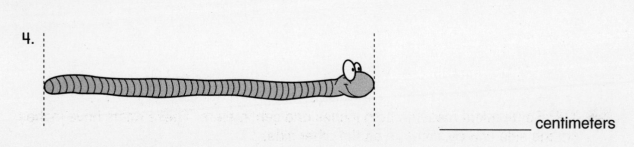

_____ centimeters

Eligible Content: M4.B.2.2.1

Weight

When you want to know how heavy an object is, you measure its **weight**. Weight can be measured in U.S. customary or metric units.

U.S. Customary Units

The most commonly used U.S. customary units of weight are **ounce**, **pound**, and **ton**.

1 ounce (oz)

A slice of bread weighs about 1 ounce.

1 pound (lb) = 16 oz

A loaf of bread weighs about 1 pound.

1 ton (T) = 2,000 lb

A compact car weighs about 1 ton.

Eligible Content: M4.B.2.2.1

Practice

Directions: For Numbers 1 through 4, write an estimate for the weight of each item using the unit given.

1. a dump truck: _____ tons

2. a telephone: _____ pounds

3. a sack of potatoes: _____ pounds

4. a ruler: _____ ounces

Directions: For Numbers 5 through 8, fill in the blank with the most reasonable U.S. customary unit of weight.

5. A blackbird weighs about 3 _____.

6. A bunch of grapes weighs about 18 _____.

7. A baby weighs about 8 _____.

8. A horse weighs about 1 _____.

9. Which is the **best** estimate for the weight of a professional football player?

    A. 40 pounds

    B. 80 pounds

    C. 100 pounds

    D. 240 pounds

10. Which is the **best** estimate for the weight of this book?

    A. 4 pounds

    B. 16 ounces

    C. 64 pounds

    D. 128 tons

Metric Units

The most commonly used metric units of weight are **gram** and **kilogram**.

1 gram (g)
A paper clip has a weight of about 1 gram.

1 kilogram (kg) = 1,000 g
A pineapple has a weight of about 1 kilogram.

 **Practice**

Directions: For Numbers 1 through 4, write an estimate for the weight of each item using the unit given.

1. an apple: _____ grams

2. a bowling ball: _____ kilograms

3. a cow: _____ kilograms

4. a rubber band: _____ grams

Directions: For Numbers 5 through 8, fill in the blank with the most reasonable metric unit of weight.

5. A parrot weighs about 250 _____.

6. A pumpkin weighs about 5 _____.

7. An orange weighs about 100 _____.

8. A dog weighs about 12 _____.

9. Which is the **best** estimate for the weight of a dictionary?

   A. 2 grams

   B. 2 kilograms

   C. 20 grams

   D. 20 kilograms

10. Which is the **best** estimate for the weight of a tennis ball?

   A. 5 grams

   B. 5 kilograms

   C. 50 grams

   D. 50 kilograms

Capacity

When you want to know how much liquid an object can hold, you measure its **capacity**. Capacity can be measured in U.S. customary or metric units. To measure capacity, you can use **measuring cups**.

U.S. Customary Units

The most commonly used U.S. customary units of capacity are **fluid ounce**, **cup**, **pint**, **quart**, and **gallon**.

1 cup (c) = 8 fluid ounces (fl oz)

A measuring cup like this has a capacity of 1 cup.

1 pint (pt) = 2 c

A drinking glass has a capacity of about 1 pint.

1 quart (qt) = 2 pt

A container of orange juice like this has a capacity of about 1 quart.

1 gallon (gal) = 4 qt

A milk jug has a capacity of about 1 gallon.

Eligible Content: M4.B.2.2.1

 **Practice**

Directions: For Numbers 1 through 4, write an estimate for the capacity of each item using the unit given.

1. a bathtub: _____ gallons

2. a coffee mug: _____ cups

3. a test tube: _____ fluid ounces

4. a blender: _____ pints

Directions: For Numbers 5 through 8, fill in the blank with the most reasonable U.S. customary unit of capacity.

5. The capacity of a large aquarium is about 50 _____.

6. The capacity of a yogurt container is about 10 _____.

7. The capacity of a small milk carton is about 1 _____.

8. The capacity of an ice cream pail is about 5 _____.

9. Which is the **best** estimate for the capacity of a kitchen sink?

    A.   2 gallons

    B.   5 gallons

    C. 18 gallons

    D. 45 gallons

10. Which is the **best** estimate for the capacity of a fishbowl?

    A.   2 cups

    B. 10 cups

    C. 50 cups

    D. 100 cups

Metric Units

The most commonly used metric units of capacity are **milliliter**, **liter**, and **kiloliter**.

1 milliliter (mL)

This eyedropper shows about 1 milliliter.

1 liter (L) = 1,000 mL

The capacity of this kind of carton is about 1 liter.

1 kiloliter (kL) = 1,000 L

The capacity of a wading pool is about 1 kiloliter.

Eligible Content: M4.B.2.2.1

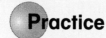 **Practice**

Directions: For Numbers 1 through 4, write an estimate for the capacity of each item using the unit given.

1. a drinking straw: _____ milliliters

2. a car's gas tank: _____ liters

3. a water jug: _____ liters

4. a water tower: _____ kiloliters

Directions: For Numbers 5 through 8, fill in the blank with the most reasonable metric unit of capacity.

5. The capacity of a paint can is about 4 _____.

6. The capacity of a cup of soup is about 200 _____.

7. The capacity of a spoonful of medicine is about 20 _____.

8. The capacity of a hot tub is about 5 _____.

9. Which is the **best** estimate for the capacity of a bottle of nail polish?

   A.   2 milliliters

   B.   20 milliliters

   C.   200 milliliters

   D. 2,000 milliliters

10. Which is the **best** estimate for the capacity of a barrel of oil?

    A. 7 milliliters

    B. 17 liters

    C. 170 liters

    D. 1,700 kiloliters

MATHEMATICS

1. Cecily drew a picture of a peanut.

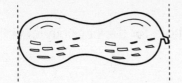

Using your ruler, what is the length of Cecily's peanut, in centimeters?

A   3

B   4

C   38

D   42

2. About how much does an adult elephant weigh?

A   350 grams

B   8,000 grams

C   50 kilograms

D   5,000 kilograms

3. John has a cookie.

Using your ruler, how long is John's cookie?

A $1\frac{1}{2}$ inches

B $1\frac{3}{4}$ inches

C   2 inches

D $2\frac{1}{4}$ inches

4. Which is the **best** estimate for the length of a lunch table?

A   2 feet

B   6 feet

C   60 feet

D   200 feet

5. About how far is Pittsburgh from Penn Hills?

A   11 inches

B   11 yards

C   11 miles

D   11 feet

6. Which is the **best** estimate for the capacity of a coffee mug?

A   2 cups

B   2 pints

C   2 quarts

D   2 gallons

7. About how much fluid can a bathtub hold?

A   55 cups

B   55 pints

C   55 quarts

D   55 gallons

STOP

Eligible Content: M4.B.1.1.1

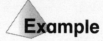

Lesson 10: Time

In this lesson, you will review telling time. You will also learn about elapsed time.

Telling Time

Time tells you what part of the day it is or how long it takes for an event to occur. Time is measured in **hours**, **minutes**, and **seconds** using a clock.

Example

This is an **analog clock**.

This is a **digital clock**.

In each day there are 24 hours. In each hour there are 60 minutes. The A.M. hours are from midnight to noon. The P.M. hours are from noon to midnight. Most analog clocks do not show whether it is A.M. or P.M. The digital clock usually has a little light next to the time to show whether it is A.M. or P.M.

On an analog clock, the short hand points to the hours, and the long hand points to the minutes. You can tell the hours by looking at the numbers around the clock. You can tell the minutes by looking at the little marks around the clock. Notice at every fifth mark there is a number. You can use that information to help you tell time on the analog clock.

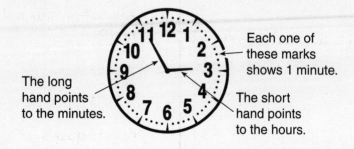

The long hand points to the minutes.

Each one of these marks shows 1 minute.

The short hand points to the hours.

If it were between midnight and noon, it would be 2:55 A.M. If it were between noon and midnight, it would be 2:55 P.M.

Example

What time does the following clock show? It is between midnight and noon.

The short hand is pointing between the 10 and 11. The hour is 10.

The long hand is pointing between the 4 and 5. Because each number represents 5 minutes, multiply 5 and 4 and add the number of marks the long hand is past the 4. It is 3 marks past the 4.

$5 \times 4 = 20$

$20 + 3 = 23$

Because it is between midnight and noon, it is 10:23 A.M.

Example

What time does the following clock show?

The light is on by the P.M., so it is 5:41 P.M.

Eligible Content: M4.B.1.1.1

Practice

Directions: For Numbers 1 through 16, write the time shown on the clock. Be sure to state whether the time is A.M. or P.M.

1. It is between midnight and noon.

_____

2. It is between midnight and noon.

_____

3. It is between noon and midnight.

_____

4. It is between noon and midnight.

_____

5. It is between midnight and noon.

_____

6. It is between noon and midnight.

_____

7.

_____

8.

_____

9.

_____

10.

_____

11.

_____

12.

_____

13.

_____

14.

_____

15.

_____

16.

_____

Eligible Content: M4.B.1.1.2

Talking About Time

Time is often informally read. Common words associated with reading times are "half past," "quarter past," and "quarter to." You can also talk about time as before or after an hour.

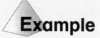 **Example**

What are three ways to say the time on the clock shown below?

The clock reads 2:40.

The time can be said as "40 minutes after 2," "20 minutes before 3," or "2:40."

Each 15 minutes is also a quarter of an hour. So, 15 minutes after an hour is a quarter past that hour. 15 minutes before an hour is a quarter to that hour. 30 minutes is half of 1 hour. If it is 30 minutes past an hour, it is half past that hour.

 Example

What are three other ways to say 9:45?

The time can be said as "45 minutes after nine," "15 minutes before 10," or "quarter to 10."

Practice

1. What is the time when a person says "quarter to six"? _____

2. What is the time when a person says "five after nine"? _____

3. What is the time when a person says "ten to ten"? _____

4. What is another way to say 1:20? _____

5. What is another way to say 3:45? _____

6. What is another way to say 4:35? _____

Directions: For Numbers 7 and 8, write two ways to say the time shown on each clock.

7.

_____

_____

8.

_____

_____

9. Which is the same time as "half past ten"?

   A. 10:05

   B. 10:15

   C. 10:30

   D. 10:45

10. Which is the same time as "9:15"?

    A. quarter to nine

    B. quarter past nine

    C. quarter to ten

    D. half past nine

Eligible Content: M4.B.1.1.3, M4.B.1.1.4

Elapsed Time

The time that passes from the start of an activity to the end of the activity is **elapsed time**. To find elapsed time, you need to understand hours and minutes.

 **Example**

How much time elapsed from 2:15 to 3:34?

Starting Time

Ending Time

Count how many times the long hand makes one trip all the way around the clock.

2:15 to 3:15 = one trip = 1 hour

The long hand made 1 trip around the clock. This is 1 hour.

Now count the remaining minutes. Count by fives starting at 3:15 and stopping at 3:30. Then add the last 4 minutes from 3:30 to 3:34.

There are 19 minutes between 3:15 and 3:34.

1 hour, 19 minutes elapsed from 2:15 to 3:34.

Eligible Content: M4.B.1.1.3, M4.B.1.1.4

You can use elapsed time to figure out when an activity started or ended.

**Example**

Raven left for the park at 3:30 P.M. He came home 1 hour, 20 minutes later. What time did Raven come home?

Start at 3:30. Add 1 hour.

3:30 to 4:30 = 1 hour

Now add the remaining minutes. Start at 30 and count by fives 4 times to add 20 minutes.

30, 35, 40, 45, 50

Raven came home from the park at 4:50 P.M.

Eligible Content: M4.B.1.1.3, M4.B.1.1.4

Practice

1. Sheila arrived at the party at the time shown on the digital clock on the left. She left the party at the time shown on the digital clock on the right.

Arrived　　　　　　　　　　　　Left

How long was Sheila at the party? _____

2. Zach left his house at 11:10 A.M. and arrived at his grandmother's house at 12:48 P.M.

Left　　　　　　　　　　　　Arrived

How long did Zach's trip take? _____

3. Johnny left his house at 10:40 A.M. and arrived at Philadelphia International Airport at 11:52 A.M.

Left　　　　　　　　　　　　Arrived

How long did it take Johnny to get to Philadelphia International Airport?

_____

4. Matt's basketball game starts at the time shown on this clock.

Matt's coach wants the team to arrive at the gym 30 minutes before the game starts. It takes Matt 20 minutes to ride his bike from his house to the gym. What is the latest time that Matt can leave home and still arrive at the gym when his coach wants him to?

_____

5. Morgan started practicing her clarinet at the time shown on this clock.

Morgan practiced her clarinet for 48 minutes. What time did Morgan finish practicing?

_____

6. Kiah drove 25 minutes from Erie to Waterford. She arrived in Waterford at 2:55 P.M. What time did Kiah leave Erie?

_____

7. Laura arrived at tumbling class at 4:45 P.M. The class was 1 hour, 5 minutes long. What time did the class end?

_____

8. Vanessa arrived at the store at 3:30 P.M. and got home at 4:25 P.M. How long was Vanessa at the store?

_____

MATHEMATICS

1. Grant started reading a book at the time shown on the clock below.

Which digital clock shows the same time? (It is between noon and midnight.)

A

B

C

D

2. Which is one way to say 7:15?

  A quarter after seven

  B quarter until seven

  C quarter after eight

  D quarter until eight

3. Lulu arrived at the video arcade at 3:55 P.M. She left the arcade at 4:45 P.M. How long was Lulu at the arcade?

  A 10 minutes

  B 40 minutes

  C 50 minutes

  D 70 minutes

4. Evan's soccer game began at 9:25 A.M. The game lasted 1 hour, 15 minutes. What time did the game end?

  A 8:10 A.M.

  B 9:40 A.M.

  C 10:40 A.M.

  D 10:50 A.M.

5. Spencer spent 50 minutes at the library. He left the library at the time shown on the clock.

What time did Spencer arrive at the library?

  A 3:10

  B 3:40

  C 4:10

  D 4:40

6. Brady arrived at the Children's Museum of Pittsburgh at 12:10 P.M. He left at 1:38 P.M.

> **A.** Draw the hands on the clocks below to show when Brady arrived and left the museum.
>
>
>
> Arrived   Left

> **B.** How long was Brady at the museum? Explain how you found your answer.

STOP

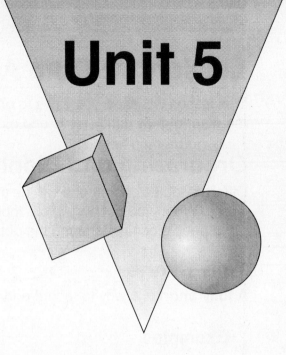

Unit 5

Data Analysis and Probability

By organizing data, you can find out things such as how many of your classmates like to go hiking, who read the most books over summer vacation, or what kinds of vegetables your friends like to eat (if any). Probability is a way of predicting and showing all the possible ways that an event can turn out.

In this unit, you will review how to organize, display, and understand data in tables and graphs. You will also review how to find the likelihood that an event will happen.

In This Unit

Eligible Content: M4.E.1.1.1

Lesson 11: Data Analysis

This lesson will show you ways to organize and display sets of data. You will then use the data to draw conclusions and make predictions.

Organizing and Displaying Data

Different tables and graphs can help you organize and display data in a way that makes sense. When you put data into a table or graph, be sure to label the table or graph so other people can understand the data.

Tally Charts

A **tally chart** is a way to record and organize data as you collect it.

Example

Tina asked her classmates about their favorite places to visit in Philadelphia. She put her data into the following tally chart.

Favorite Philadelphia Places

Place	Tally	Number of Students
Liberty Bell	ЖИТ	5
Franklin Institute	ЖИТ II	7
Penn's Landing	IIII	4
Philadelphia Zoo	II	2
Independence Hall	II	2

Practice

Directions: Use the tally chart above to answer Numbers 1 through 4.

1. How many students in Tina's class chose Penn's Landing? _____

2. How many students in Tina's class chose the zoo? _____

3. What place did the most students choose? _____

4. Shantel was absent when the survey was done. Based on the other answers, what do you predict her favorite place in Philadelphia would be?

_____

Eligible Content: M4.E.1.1.1, M4.E.1.2.1, M4.E.1.2.2

Pictographs

A **pictograph** uses pictures or symbols to show data. The key will show you what each picture represents. The title of a pictograph is chosen by identifying the topic of the data.

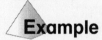 **Example**

Maya and her dad went bass fishing on Lake Erie. The following pictograph shows how many bass they caught each day.

Bass Caught

Wednesday	🐟 🐟 🐟
Thursday	🐟 🐟 🐟 🐟
Friday	🐟 🐟 🐟 🐟 🐟 🐟
Saturday	🐟 🐟

KEY
🐟 = 2 fish

Each 🐟 stands for 2 fish. How many bass did Maya and her dad catch on Wednesday?

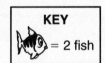

$$🐟 + 🐟 + 🐟 = 2 + 2 + 2 = 6$$

Maya and her dad caught 6 bass on Wednesday.

Practice

Directions: Use the pictograph above to answer Numbers 1 through 4.

1. On what day did Maya and her dad catch the most bass? _____

2. On what day did Maya and her dad catch exactly 4 bass? _____

3. How many more bass did Maya and her dad catch on Friday than on Wednesday?

_____

4. How many bass did Maya and her dad catch in all? _____

Directions: Use the following information to answer Numbers 5 through 7.

Renee asked each of the students in her class what his or her favorite city in Pennsylvania is. Here are the results of her survey:

Allentown, Harrisburg, Harrisburg, Pittsburgh, York, Allentown, Pittsburgh, Pittsburgh, Allentown, York, Pittsburgh, Harrisburg, Pittsburgh, York, York, Pittsburgh, Harrisburg, Pittsburgh, Pittsburgh, Harrisburg, Pittsburgh, Harrisburg, Pittsburgh

5. Fill in the following tally chart with Renee's data.

Favorite Pennsylvania Cities

City	Tally	Number of Students
Allentown		
Harrisburg		
Pittsburgh		
York		

6. Complete the pictograph of the data. Make a key to show what each picture represents.

Favorite Pennsylvania Cities

City	Number of Students
Allentown	
Harrisburg	
Pittsburgh	
York	

KEY

7. Explain why you chose the picture and the key that you used for the pictograph.

_____

_____

Eligible Content: M4.E.1.1.1, M4.E.1.2.1, M4.E.1.2.2

Bar Graphs

A **bar graph** uses thick bars to show data. Bar graphs are used to compare amounts of similar things.

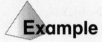 **Example**

The following bar graph shows the number of students who prefer each of four Pennsylvania teams.

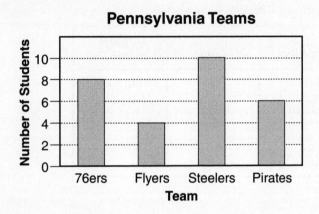

Pennsylvania Teams

 Practice

Directions: Use the bar graph above to answer Numbers 1 through 5.

1. How many students prefer the Steelers? _____

2. Which team do exactly 8 students prefer? _____

3. How many more students prefer the Pirates than the Flyers? _____

4. If each student prefers only one team, how many students are in the bar graph altogether?

   _____

5. If one more student is asked what his or her favorite Pennsylvania team is, what do you predict his or her answer will be? Explain your answer.

   _____

   _____

Directions: Use the following information to answer Numbers 6 through 9.

At Riley's family reunion, Riley kept track of the color of each person's eyes. Here are the results of his count:

blue, blue, green, brown, brown, hazel, blue, blue, brown, green, hazel, hazel, green, brown, blue, blue, blue, green, hazel, brown, green, blue

6. Fill in the following tally chart with Riley's data.

Family Eye Color

Color	Tally	Number of People
Blue		
Green		
Brown		
Hazel		

7. Make a bar graph of the data.

Family Eye Color

8. Which two eye colors do the same number of people have? _____

_____

9. If one more person comes to the family reunion, what color do you think his or her eyes will be? Explain your answer.

_____

_____

Line Graphs

A **line graph** is used to show how data change over a period of time.

Example

The line graph shows the amount in sales the Comic Connection made over a 10-week period.

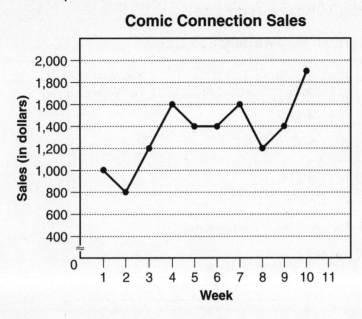

Comic Connection Sales

Practice

Directions: Use the line graph above to answer Numbers 1 through 4.

1. Between what two weeks in a row was there no change in weekly sales?

   _____

2. Between what two weeks in a row was there the biggest increase in sales?

   _____

3. What is the amount of increase in sales from week 1 to week 10? _____

4. Do you think the amount in sales for week 11 will be higher or lower than for week 10? Explain your answer.

   _____

   _____

Eligible Content: M4.E.1.2.1, M4.E.1.2.2

Translating Data

You can represent the same data in more than one type of graph.

 **Example**

Four friends play on the same softball team. They made the following pictograph to show how many hits each of them had this season.

Softball Players' Hits

Tina	🥎 🥎 🥎 🥎 🥎
Shannon	🥎 🥎 ◖
Anna	🥎 🥎 🥎 ◖
Christina	🥎 🥎

KEY	
🥎	= 10 hits
◖	= 5 hits

This data can also be shown in a bar graph.

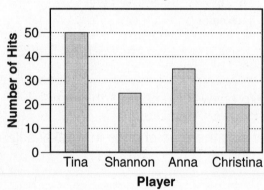

Softball Players' Hits

The graphs look different, but the data are the same. They both show that Tina had 50 hits, Shannon had 25 hits, Anna had 35 hits, and Christina had 20 hits.

Practice

Directions: Use the following information and graph to answer Numbers 1 and 2.

The fourth graders at Keystone Elementary School made the following bar graph to show what kinds of pets they have.

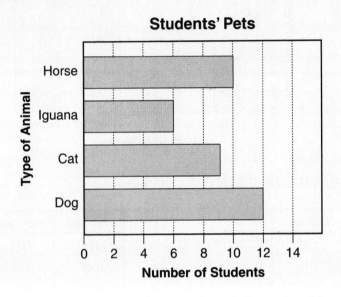

1. Complete the pictograph below with the data from the bar graph.

Students' Pets

Horse	
Iguana	
Cat	
Dog	

KEY

2. Explain why you chose the picture and the key that you used.

_____

_____

MATHEMATICS

1. Kevin kept track of the vehicles that drove past his house one afternoon. His results are shown in the following bar graph.

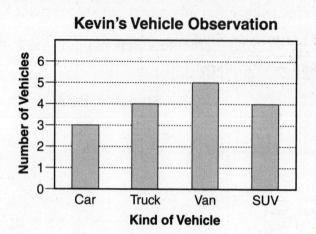

Which tally chart correctly displays Kevin's data?

A

Vehicle	Number
Car	⊪⊓
Truck	III
Van	IIII
SUV	IIII

B

Vehicle	Number
Car	IIII
Truck	IIII
Van	III
SUV	⊪⊓

C

Vehicle	Number
Car	IIII
Truck	⊪⊓
Van	III
SUV	IIII

D

Vehicle	Number
Car	III
Truck	IIII
Van	⊪⊓
SUV	IIII

MATHEMATICS

2. The pictograph below shows how many glasses of lemonade were sold by Bo, Carrie, Scott, and Vanessa.

Glasses of Lemonade Sold

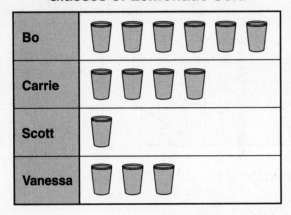

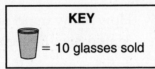

KEY

= 10 glasses sold

How many more glasses of lemonade did Carrie sell than Scott?

A   3

B   4

C   30

D   40

3. The line graph below shows how many pounds of paper were collected from January to March.

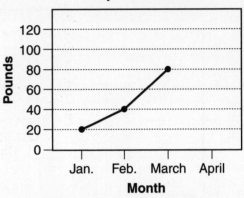

The pattern continues. Based on the graph, how many pounds of paper should be expected to be collected by April?

A   80

B   100

C   120

D   140

4. The bar graph below shows how many hours Rob practiced his tuba over the week.

Rob's Tuba Practice

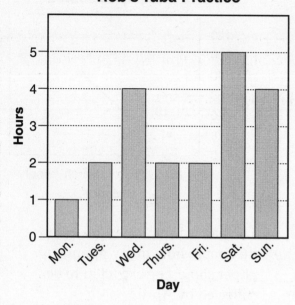

How many hours did Rob practice his tuba altogether?

A   7

B   20

C   22

D   28

5. The line graph below shows how many bikes Bob's Bike Shop sold from January through April.

Bob's Bike Shop

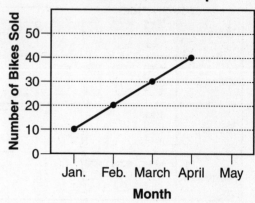

How many more bikes were sold in March than in January?

A   10

B   20

C   30

D   40

MATHEMATICS

6. Mr. Jay's fourth-grade class recorded each student's hair color. Here are their results:

brown, blonde, blonde, black, red, black, brown, brown, blonde, brown, black, red, brown, blonde, brown, black, brown, brown, black, black, blonde, brown, black

---

A. Make a bar graph showing the number of students with each hair color.

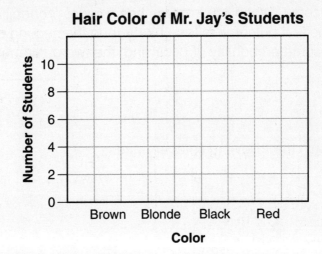

Hair Color of Mr. Jay's Students

B. How many more students have brown hair than blonde hair?

C. How many students are in Mr. Jay's class?

D. If one more student joined Mr. Jay's class, what color hair would you predict is least likely for the student to have?

STOP

Eligible Content: M4.E.3.1.1

Lesson 12: Probability

In this lesson, you will review probability and predicting the likelihood of an event.

Determining Likelihood

Probability is the chance that an event will or will not happen. When an outcome has a higher probability of occurring than another outcome, the first outcome is **more likely** than the second outcome. When an outcome has a lower probability of occurring than another outcome, the first outcome is **less likely** than the second outcome. When two outcomes have the same probability of occurring, the two outcomes are **equally likely** to occur.

Example

Julia will spin the following spinner once.

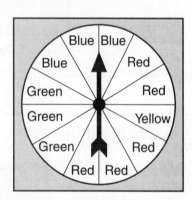

There are 5 red sections, 3 blue sections, 3 green sections, and 1 yellow section.

The spinner is **more likely** to land on red than blue because there are more red sections than blue sections.

The spinner is **less likely** to land on yellow than green because there are fewer yellow sections than green sections.

The spinner is **equally likely** to land on blue and green because there are the same number of blue and green sections.

Eligible Content: M4.E.3.1.1

You can also compare more than two outcomes. When an outcome has a higher probability of occurring than any other outcome, it is **most likely** to occur. When an outcome has a lower probability of occurring than any other outcome, it is **least likely** to occur.

 Example

Martin will spin this spinner once. Which outcome is **most likely** to occur?

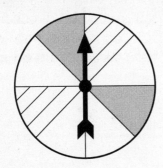

There are 4 white sections, 2 striped sections, and 2 gray sections. Since there are more white sections than any other kind, the spinner is most likely to land on a white section.

 Example

There are 20 marbles in a bag. Nine of the marbles are red, 5 are blue, 4 are clear, and 2 are green. Jenna is going to pick one marble out of the bag without looking. What color is Jenna **least likely** to pick?

Since there are fewer green marbles than any other color, Jenna is least likely to pick a green marble.

Practice

Directions: Use the bag of marbles to answer Numbers 1 through 3. One marble will be picked out of the bag without looking.

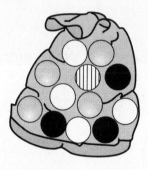

1. Which types of marbles are **equally likely** to be picked? _____

2. Which type of marble is **less likely** to be picked than a black marble?

   _____

3. How likely is it that a white marble will be picked rather than a black marble?

   _____

Directions: Use the spinner below to answer Numbers 4 through 6. The spinner will be spun one time.

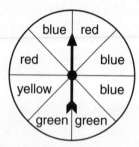

4. Which color section is **more likely** to be landed on than green? _____

5. Which color section is **less likely** to be landed on than red? _____

6. How likely is it that the spinner will land on yellow rather than green?

   _____

Eligible Content: M4.E.3.1.1

Directions: Use the following information to answer Numbers 7 through 10.

Harry has a bag of crayons: 7 crayons are red, 8 are blue, 3 are yellow, and 2 are green. He will pick one crayon from the bag without looking.

7. What color crayon is **most likely** to be picked? _____

8. What color crayon is **least likely** to be picked? _____

9. What colors of crayon are **more likely** to be picked than yellow?

    _____

10. What colors of crayon are **less likely** to be picked than red?

    _____

Directions: Use the spinner below to answer Numbers 11 through 14. The spinner will be spun one time.

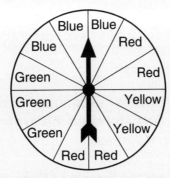

11. Which color section is **most likely** to be landed on? _____

12. Which color section is **least likely** to be landed on? _____

13. Which color sections are **equally likely** to be landed on?

    _____

14. Which of the following is **more likely**: landing on yellow or landing on blue? Explain your answer.

    _____

    _____

Predicting Outcomes

You can **predict** the results of a probability experiment if you know how likely it is that each possible outcome will occur. You can test your predictions by actually doing the experiment.

You can make new predictions based on the results of your probability experiment. Then you can test the new predictions by repeating the experiment.

 **Example**

Tangela predicted the outcomes of a probability experiment in which she will flip a coin 100 times.

Since there are 2 equally likely outcomes, she predicted that the coin would land heads up 50 times and tails up 50 times.

The following table shows the results of Tangela's experiment.

Result	Number of Outcomes
Heads	55
Tails	45

Tangela used the results of her experiment to make a new prediction. She predicted that the next time she does the experiment, the coin will land heads up 55 times and tails up 45 times.

The following table shows the results of Tangela's second experiment.

Result	Number of Outcomes
Heads	49
Tails	51

You can see that Tangela's predictions and results are not exactly the same. However, you should also notice that the predictions and results are close to each other.

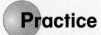 **Practice**

Directions: For Numbers 1 through 11, you will be doing a probability experiment. In the experiment, you will roll a number cube numbered 1 through 6 twenty-four times and record the outcomes.

1. When you roll a number cube labeled 1 through 6, what are the possible outcomes?

   _____

2. Are there any outcomes that are more likely to occur than others? Are there any outcomes less likely to occur than others?

   _____

   _____

3. For each possible outcome you wrote down in Number 1, predict how many times out of twenty-four that outcome will occur.

   _____

   _____

4. Roll the number cube twenty-four times. Write the outcomes in the following tables.

Roll	1	2	3	4	5	6	7	8	9	10	11	12
Outcome												

Roll	13	14	15	16	17	18	19	20	21	22	23	24
Outcome												

5. How many times did the number cube land on each possible outcome?

   _____

   _____

6. How close were the results of your experiment to your prediction?

    _____

    _____

7. Use the results of your experiment to predict how many times out of twenty-four each outcome will occur if you do the experiment again.

    _____

    _____

8. Do the experiment again. Roll the number cube twenty-four times. Write the outcomes in the following tables.

Roll	1	2	3	4	5	6	7	8	9	10	11	12
Outcome												

Roll	13	14	15	16	17	18	19	20	21	22	23	24
Outcome												

9. How many times did the number cube land on each possible outcome?

    _____

    _____

10. How close were the results of your second experiment to your prediction?

    _____

    _____

11. How close were the results of your second experiment to your first experiment?

    _____

    _____

MATHEMATICS

1. These 10 word cards were placed into a box. Alex will pick a card from the box without looking.

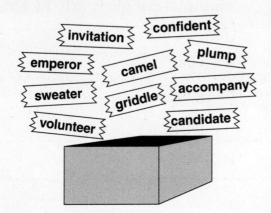

What letter is the word Alex will pick **most likely** to start with?

A   C

B   I

C   P

D   S

2. If the spinner is spun once, it is **equally likely** to land on which two shapes?

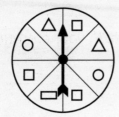

A   ○   △

B   □   ▭

C   ○   □

D   △   ▭

3. If the spinner is spun once, what is the likelihood that it will land on a section numbered 4 rather than a section numbered 3?

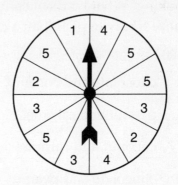

A   more likely

B   less likely

C   equally likely

D   most likely

4. What is the likelihood that Dustin will pick a black marble rather than a gray marble from the bag below?

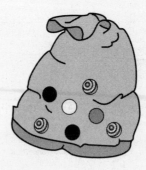

A   most likely

B   less likely

C   more likely

D   equally likely

5. A box of candy contains 9 chocolate pieces, 3 coconut pieces, 6 peanut pieces, and 2 caramel pieces. Carol will pick a piece of candy without looking. What kinds of candy is Carol **more likely** to pick than a coconut piece?

A   chocolate and coconut

B   peanut and caramel

C   coconut and caramel

D   chocolate and peanut

6. A bag contains 5 blue marbles, 3 purple marbles, 6 green marbles, and 4 red marbles. Which color marble is **least likely** to be picked from the bag?

A   blue

B   green

C   purple

D   red

STOP